Parmenter

ep sport

Basketball Techniques

ep sport

Basketball Techniques

Brian Coleman & Peter Ray

A & C Black · London

First published 1987 by A & C Black
(Publishers) Limited, 35 Bedford Row,
London WC1R 4JH

© 1987 Brian Coleman and Peter Ray

ISBN 0 7136 5575 5

Coleman, Brian
    Basketball techniques.—(EP sport)
    1. Basketball
    I. Title   II. Ray, Peter   III. Series
    796.32′32   GV885
    ISBN 0-7136-5575-5

Printed and bound in Great Britain by
R. J. Acford, Chichester

CONTENTS

INTRODUCTION

In recent years more and more people have gained pleasure from playing, coaching or watching basketball. The authors believe that enjoyment for the game can come from a greater understanding of the sport and have focused their attention on an appreciation of its techniques and tactics.

This book, written for the basketball player, has given an opportunity to present up-to-date ideas on the basic skills of the game and to explain the principles of attacking and defensive play.

Basketball is one of the most popular sports in the world, with over 160 countries affiliated to FIBA, the International Basketball Association. Its popularity is due to the simplicity of the rules and to the athleticism and skill of the participants. It is a game of action: play moves rapidly from one end of the court to the other as the teams attack and counter-attack in an effort to win a game that is frequently decided by one basket.

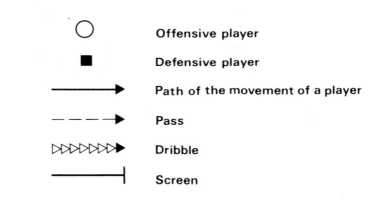

Offensive player
Defensive player
Path of the movement of a player
Pass
Dribble
Screen

Offensive play –
front court

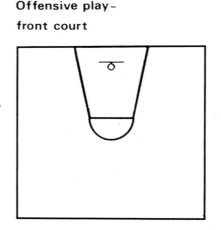

Defensive play –
back court

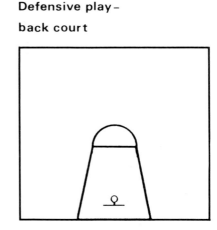

Figure 1 *Key to the diagrams and symbols used in this book*

Although the text is in the masculine gender and our illustrations show mostly male players, the game is enjoyed equally by both sexes, and by young and old.

Basketball is a game of attack and defence; each component affects the other. The way the attacking team plays is influenced by, or can influence, the defensive team. The two parts of the game are closely related but in the analysis of techniques and tactics within this book it is sometimes necessary to isolate one or other component. The interdependence of attack and defence is one of the fascinations of the game. The play is constantly changing.

Ultimately, it is the basic techniques and team skills covered in this book that form the sound basis for every successful basketball team. The important difference between the beginner and the international player is that the latter can perform the fundamentals of the game very well. This book aims to give coaches, teachers and players insights into these fundamentals in order to produce both the skilful basketball individual and team.

1 THE GAME OF BASKETBALL

THE BASIC GAME

Basketball is a simple game. Primarily, it is a team passing game, played with the hands, with the object of scoring in a horizontal target which is 45 cm (18 in.) in diameter and suspended 3.15 m (10 ft 4 in.) from the floor. The game is played to three basic rules: no contact, no running while holding the ball and one continuous dribble only. It encourages maximum participation—no player on either team is restricted from getting the ball whenever it is in play, and the players are free to occupy any part of the playing area not already occupied by an opponent. Each player can shoot from any position on the playing court. The popularity of the game can be traced to this essential simplicity, which enables all players to do everything. Basketball was invented in 1891 by a Canadian, James Naismith, who wanted a game anyone could play and enjoy. The enthusiasm for the sport today is an indication of his success.

THE BASIC RULES

The official rules of basketball, which have been written to control the game at international level, may appear complex, but in essence they are relatively straightforward. To understand the rules it is easier to look at them under two headings, Rules of Play and Rules of Administration.

Rules of Play

The three basic rules of playing the game have already been mentioned. These are 'no contact', 'one pace' and 'one dribble'.

No contact It is the duty of every player on court to avoid contacting another player, but it is accepted that with ten players moving rapidly in a confined space contact will occur. The officials are charged with the duty of making a judgement on contact and of penalising it by calling a foul. Every player on court is entitled to occupy any part of the court not occupied by an opponent, provided that he does not make any personal contact in obtaining that position. A player is considered to occupy not only the part of the floor covered by his feet, but also a 'cylinder' between the floor and the roof, with a base roughly equivalent to the player's body dimensions. Should an opponent run or reach into this 'cylinder' and cause contact, then he is held responsible for the foul.

One pace while holding the ball A player is not permitted to carry the ball when moving for more than one complete pace. When coming to a stop with the ball a player can use a two-count rhythm (see page 16). A player having come to a stop may pivot, that is, step once, or more than once, in any direction with the same foot, while the other foot, the pivot foot, is kept at its point of contact with the floor. The player may lift the pivot foot when making a pass or taking a shot, but he must have released the ball by the time the pivot foot is again grounded.

One dribble The dribble in basketball is the method used to move, with the ball under control, from one spot to another. A dribble is a continuous bouncing action using either hand, but not both simultaneously. The dribble ends when the ball comes to rest in one or both hands. Once the player has stopped his dribble, he is not permitted to dribble again until the ball has been touched by another player.

RULES OF ADMINISTRATION

Start The game is started at the beginning of each half with a jump-ball between two opponents at the centre circle. The official throws the ball up between the two players.

Restart after a score After a basket has been scored, the game is restarted by a member of the team which has had the basket scored against it taking the ball out of court at the end line and making a pass into court.

Restart after a violation of the rules After the referee has stopped play because of a violation of the rules, the game will usually be restarted by the team against which the offence has been committed. The ball will be taken out of court at the side at the nearest point to where the

infraction occurred, and play will be restarted with a pass into court.

The basic simplicity of the game has led to it being adapted for play by the disabled from wheelchairs. Basketball has also been adapted for children under 12 years of age by using a smaller ball and a lower basket. This game of Mini Basketball encourages boys and girls to learn and enjoy the sport, and provides an opportunity for children to develop the basic skills of the game. An important part of the Mini Basketball philosophy is that children should be encouraged to officiate their own games.

Wheelchair basketball

PLAYING POSITIONS

The player's position in the team will depend upon his own skill, that of his team-mates, his height in relation to other members of the team and the tactics the coach decides to employ. In basketball the name given to a player's position is determined by the area of the court taken up when his team is on the attack. There are three basic court playing positions: guard, forward and pivot. These playing areas are illustrated in Figure 2.

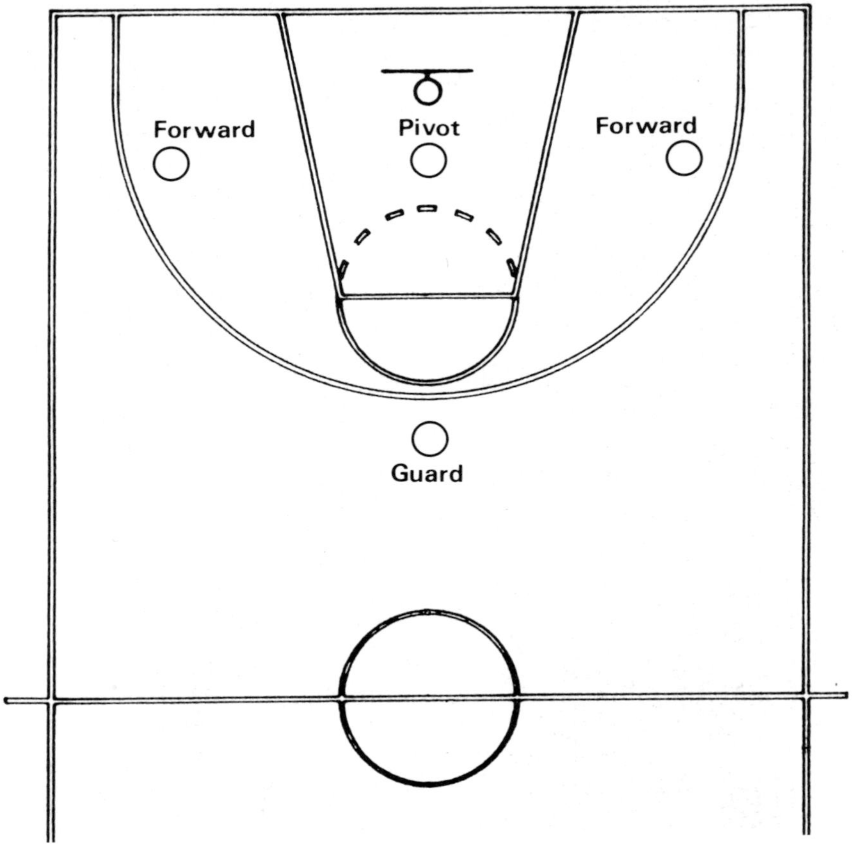

Guard

A player who plays in a guard position will, when his team is on attack, normally operate in the area of court between the centre line and the free-throw line

Figure 2 *The basic positions*

extended to the side lines. He will usually be one of the smaller players in the team and will be responsible for bringing the ball up court to start the team's attack. He will need to be a good driver and a capable shooter from the $4\frac{1}{2}$–$7\frac{1}{2}$ metre (15–25 ft) range from the basket. He is the player likely to attempt the 3 point shots.

A talented guard will be able to use his drive to move close to the basket, not necessarily for a shot but to draw the defence to himself, and will then pass off to a team-mate in a better position for the shot. This demands that he is a very good passer of the ball and capable of 'reading' the movements of team-mates so that he passes them the ball as they break free.

The player who takes the guard position is frequently one of the more experienced players, because from this position he will direct his team's attacking play. For this reason he may be referred to as a 'playmaker' or, using an American Football term, a 'quarterback'.

A team may employ either one or two guards in its attacking alignment. When two guards are used one of these will often undertake the direction of play and he can be referred to as the 'point guard'; his partner may then be called the 'off guard'. When a team uses a one-guard attack this player can also be called the 'point guard'.

Forward

The forwards play on attack in the area of the court, either on the right- or left-hand side, between the restricted area and the side lines. They will be among the taller players in the team, will have a good drive and will be able to shoot well from the corners and sides of the court. They must be prepared to set screens to help free a team-mate for a drive or shot. A forward must also be prepared to move in to gain attacking rebounds should a shot be missed.

Pivot

The player selected to play in a pivot position is usually the tallest player in the team and plays close to the basket. A pivot player will be expected to have the following skills: the ability to make a good shot close to the basket (usually under pressure from close marking opponents); the possession of good footwork so that he can free himself in the area under the basket to receive a pass and, having received it, to move in for a shot; the ability to hold a close-to-basket position once gained; and the capacity to rebound strongly.

When a team uses two pivot players one will play near the free-throw line in a 'high' position and the other near the base line in a 'low' position. (Part of a team's attacking play can involve these two players exchanging positions.) A player in the pivot position may also be referred to as a post player. The term 'post position' is often used for a player who takes up a high position near the free-throw line, with his back to the basket.

These positions are by no means rigid and as the team's attacking play develops so a guard may have to play from a forward position. However, an inexperienced player will find it easier to understand his role in the team's attack if he is operating from a specific court position.

The number of players that a team uses in each position can be varied, and will depend upon the tactics selected by the coach. Good use of players will ensure a balanced spacing in the front court and will mean that team members do not get in each other's way. It also ensures that sufficient players are positioned with responsiblity to move in for the attacking rebound and to delay the opponent's outlet pass.

One or two players stationed in the guard position will give defensive cover against possible

fast breaks, and will be in a position to receive a pass when an attacking play breaks down. To describe the way players are organised on attack a 'shorthand' is used in which the number of players in each playing position on court is stated. For example, an attack with two guards, two

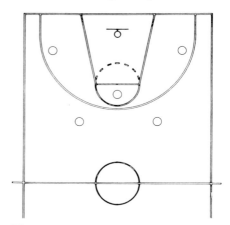

Figure 3 *2–1–2 formation*

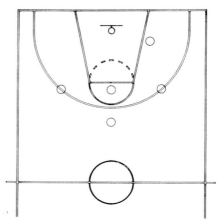

Figure 4 *1–3–1 formation*

forwards (one on each side of the court) and one pivot player would be referred to as a 2—1—2 formation. This is illustrated in Figure 3. Another commonly used formation is 1—3—1 in which a team plays with one guard, two forward and two pivot players. It is illustrated in Figure 4.

A player can occupy any position on court and will find himself fully involved in attack and defence. This means that on the change of possession a player will move with the other players from one end of the court to the other. The defensive position he adopts will

Basic defensive stance

depend upon the tactics being employed by the coach. If the team is playing a man-to-man defence, a player should ideally mark an opponent of his own size, speed and ability. If he is playing guard when on attack, he is likely to find himself marking an opposing guard. However, if the team is employing a zone defence, the taller, defensive players will normally be used closest to the basket being defended, and the smaller, faster players will be away from the basket.

BASIC TEAM PLAY

Team play in basketball involves the application of ideas which are very similar to those used in other team games: for example, safe passing, spreading out when on attack, movement of the ball and/or players, and passing and moving into open space for the return pass. An understanding of the basic ingredients is important for successful development of team play and some main points will be considered before individual techniques and skills are analysed in more detail in later chapters.

Defending

The simplest defence used in the game is for a defensive player to be responsible for one opponent and to aim to limit the attacking options of that opponent. The basic defensive position should be taken

up between the attacking player and the basket that is being defended, so that the attacker has to dribble round the defender to take a close-to-basket shot. The defender will adjust his position as the attacking opponent moves, endeavouring to keep a position between opponent and basket. When defending away from the ball a player adjusts his position in relation to the ball and player movement, but still tries to maintain a position between opponent and basket.

Use of Space

In the limited area of a basketball court the correct use of space is important. The attacking team will attempt to spread out so that there is $3\frac{1}{2}$—$4\frac{1}{2}$ metres (12—15 ft) between each attacking player. At this range the attackers can make fast, accurate passes, committing each defender to mark two attacking players, and making it difficult for two defenders to mark the one attacking player with the ball. The attacking team, as it builds up its attack, will try to keep the under-basket area free; this is the area from which a higher percentage of shots can be scored.

The defensive team will also be concerned with the use of space and will endeavour to deny the attacking team the domination of that area of the court from which players are most likely to score, that is, the under-basket area. The defensive team will also try to counter any spreading out by the attacking team by employing tactics that give depth to the defence. Such depth is obtained by 'sagging'. This occurs when a defender moves towards the basket and away from the attacking player he is marking. A defender will sag when the opponent he is marking either does not have the ball and is at a distance from the ball handler or is out of scoring range. Through sagging a defender gives cover and can mark any opponent should one manage to get free near the basket.

Movement

The simplest attacking play in basketball is the pass to a team-mate and movement towards the basket looking for a return pass. Beginners and inexperienced players frequently attempt to play the game too fast and make too much movement. Basketball is a game of changes in tempo; play is initially built up slowly and then rapid movement is made as a scoring chance is developed. Part of the slow build-up could be movement of the ball from one attacking position to another.

Control

Since basketball is a 'no contact' game, emphasis should be placed on controlled movements about the court. A player should only make a movement when he has himself and the ball under control.

Time and Distance

Although the equation time = distance is not scientific, it forms the basis of an important idea, i.e. the time a player has in which to perform a skill will depend upon the distance he is from an opponent, and the faster he reacts to a situation the less distance he will require. A defender marking between the opponent and the basket he is defending gives himself sufficient space so that he has enough time to react to the opponent's movement. If he is marking an opponent closely, he will find he has less time in which to follow his movements.

An important skill is the ability to see a game situation as it develops. If the player recognises the situation, he will respond more quickly and will, therefore, need less space in which to operate than a player who is slower or who fails to notice important developments. The player who has superior appreciation of the game is likely to have an advantage over the player who has good technique but who lacks understanding.

Shooting on the Run

Although the attacking team may have moved a player with the ball free under the basket, their efforts may be of no use if that player takes too long to take the shot and thus gives the defence time to recover. To overcome this problem inexperienced players need to develop the ability to shoot on the run, that is, to perform a lay-up shot, early in their learning of the game.

Basic Basketball Stance

Control of and ability with the ball will depend on a player having proper balance and good body control. The basic basketball stance is with feet spread approximately shoulder width apart, flat on the floor and with one foot slightly ahead of the other; the knees are bent and the hips slightly flexed. The head should be up and over the base established by the feet, with the weight slightly forward and evenly distributed on to both feet.

This is the basic stance for both attacking and defensive play, and from the position the player is ready to move immediately. The illustration shows a player with the ball taking up the stance; note that the ball is held under the chin in front of the chest. From here he can shoot, start a dribble or pass. This is called the 'triple threat' position. (Note that the player is looking at the basket.)

Opposite Shooting on the move

Basic attacking stance

Footwork

The rules of the game are such that footwork is an important area of skill that players will need to develop, in particular the ability to stop with the ball and to pivot.

There are two ways of stopping when receiving a pass or when picking the ball up at the end of a dribble. Players should be able to execute both methods, the jump stop and the stride stop, equally well.

The jump stop

The stride stop

16

Jump stop The player takes the ball in the air and lands on both feet simultaneously, with feet at least shoulder width apart. The knees flex on landing to cushion the player and to prevent him overbalancing forwards. This stop is valuable because there is no commitment to a pivot foot on landing. Since it has been made on both feet, either may be selected to be the pivot foot, depending upon the game situation. This type of stop will be used by a player moving away from the basket to receive the ball or a player who is moving towards the basket to take a jump shot. Here one foot, on the same side as the shooting hand, is usually slightly ahead of the other.

Stride stop This stop is performed using a 'one, two' rhythm. The ball is received when both feet are off the floor, one foot touches the floor, then the trailing foot strides forwards and lands to execute the stop. The first foot to touch is the 'count one' and the second foot is the 'count two' in the stopping rhythm. To prevent further forward movement the stopping stride should be slightly longer than normal and contact with the floor should be made with a flat-footed action, with the knees bent.

Pivoting The pivot is closely linked with stopping, as the type of stop used will influence the variety of pivot options. If the jump stop can

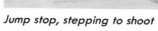
Jump stop, stepping to shoot

be mastered, it has the advantage of giving a choice of pivot foot, enabling the player to move either the left or right foot to take advantage of the way the opponent is playing or of the game situation. The stride stop will restrict a player to just one option, as only the 'one' count foot, usually the rear, can be used as the pivot foot. The pivot should be made utilising the basic basketball stance, that is, knees and hips flexed, head up. In the illustration the player has come to a jump stop at the end of a dribble; he then steps once, using the right foot as a pivot foot, to take a lay-up shot. Players need to practise the use of the pivot to move around an opponent when dribbling or to create space for a shot or pass.

A forward who has moved out to receive a pass should look to turn inwards (towards the centre of the court) by pivoting on his left foot, at the same time moving his right foot into the normal shooting position, with knees flexed and slightly apart. This will enable him to shoot (as illustrated) or drive towards the basket. If closely marked, the forward may be able to step past his defender on the 'outside' by performing a rear pivot, thereby creating space for a base-line drive.

When a player receives the ball he should pivot to face the basket

2 INDIVIDUAL BASIC SKILLS

To be a successful basketball player requires the mastery of a number of basic skills. There are four things that a player can do with a basketball: catch it, pass it, dribble it, or shoot the ball towards the basket. This chapter will consider these four individual skills, both when players are attacking and defending.

Before isolating specific techniques and skills for closer study we would remind the reader that the play of an individual occurs within the context of the full game of basketball and this involves team-mates and opponents. The skills are closely interrelated and should be practised and perfected both in training and within the game. Each technique is described and its use in the game illustrated. The order we have selected is not intended to represent any special emphasis, although we have put 'getting free' first because we believe this skill is a weakness of English basketball.

Moving Free to Receive a Pass

In the game where defenders are marking the attacking players on a man-to-man basis, a player should expect to be marked by a defender who stands between him and the basket. To develop as a member of a team a player needs to learn to free himself from the defender so that he can receive a pass. If a player has taken up an attacking position as a guard, forward or pivot, and is within twenty feet of the basket, he should now consider whether he is free to receive a pass. If so, he should be signalling for the ball. If there is space nearer the basket in which to receive a pass the player should consider how to move into it. It may be possible to get free by speed alone, beating the opponent with a quick start as the defender tries to move backwards. Here it is vital that the attacking player starts from a good basic stance, with knees bent; the quick start is useful

against an opponent who is poorly positioned with straight legs.

If the attacking player is marked by a defender who has a good position and stance, it is still possible for the attacker to lose the opponent and open the passing lane. To do this he will need to assess the reaction of the defender to certain movements. To free himself for a pass a player may make one or a combination of the following movements:

1 Move towards the ball as in the illustration on page 20.

2 Move away from the ball and then towards the ball holder to receive in the space created by the movement away from the ball.

3 Move towards the basket and then move back out to receive the ball. This move is frequently used in the game and in the illustration the player in the dark vest, number 6, steps to the basket, then changes direction and moves out to receive the ball.

Move to the ball to get free

Move towards the basket and then move out to become free to receive the ball

The forward (number 6) has stepped out and away from the defender to enable a safe pass to be made, but he could have feinted: when the defender moved out to try to continue to overplay the passing lane, the forward could have cut 'backdoor' as described below and illustrated on this page.

4 Use of a change of direction and change of speed—in particular changing speed from slow to fast (walking to running).

In the attacking area, a player must learn to get free to receive the pass so that when he receives the ball he is in a position to threaten to shoot, drive to basket past the defender, or pass to a team-mate near the basket. It is comparatively easy to move free to receive a pass, but in so doing the offensive option of the shot may be given up by moving away from the high percentage scoring area. Players need to be able to free themselves and receive the ball within a good percentage shooting area, or at least an area where the defender will be tempted to commit himself because he thinks the players may shoot.

Backdoor

If the opponent is watching the ball, it may be possible to run past him on the outside and get free. As illustrated, while the opponent watches the ball, the player in the dark vest breaks free towards the

Backdoor cut

basket, receives the ball and shoots. This cut on the side of the opponent away from the ball is called a 'backdoor' play.

The backdoor play will also be used when the defender, in an effort to intercept the ball, moves from his position between the attacker and the basket and 'overplays' the passing lane. In this instance the attacking player fakes to move to the ball, then quickly changes direction and cuts to basket, signalling for the ball.

Change of Direction

If the opponent does react to the move, the attacking player can attempt to beat him by using a sudden change of direction. The illustration shows the attacking player (number 6) starting to move to his right; as the defender adjusts to cover this move he changes direction, pushing off his outside (right) foot to cut inside to the attacking player's left and to receive the pass. As this method of getting free involves a change of direction the player will also use a change of speed, slow to fast. The initial move, the fake, should be at walking pace, with the rapid move started with the push off the outside foot. Remember to move to the attacking player's left: he will push hard off his right foot.

A roll

An alternative method of changing direction is to use a roll. A player attempts to move past his opponent to the outside, in this case to go to the baseline; as the opponent moves to cover, the attacking player stops, pivots on his inside foot and rolls, turning his back on the defender, and breaks to receive a pass.

The defender will react to movements near the basket—a step to basket is often sufficient to 'wrong foot' an opponent; then the player can move away into space to receive a pass. The example shown on this page to illustrate the principle is one of the most commonly used moves to get free in the game of basketball. A pivot player stationed on the baseline steps to basket, then charges and moves to the free-throw line to signal for a pass from a player.

Change of direction to get free

When playing against defensive pressure, such as when a pivot player finds he is being 'fronted', i.e. the defender has taken up a position between him and the ball, the pivot player should step to basket and signal for a high lob pass over the defender by a team-mate.

Upon receiving the ball, when it has been passed to a pivot player who has been overplayed, the pivot will look to make a power move to basket for the shot. This power move can be made either with or without a one-bounce dribble. If the dribble is used, it should be made between the legs to give protection to the ball. The pivot player can make use of a roll to obtain a position close to basket, with the defender on his back, thus creating a passing lane and putting him in a good position.

In all the situations illustrated with a pivot player moving free the player uses his footwork to gain an advantageous position, placing the opponent 'on his back'.

A roll

Post player (in black) fakes low and then moves high to receive the pass

Beating overplay by the defender

Making a power move to the basket for the shot

PASSING AND CATCHING

Signalling

Signalling is vital if the player is to develop an understanding with the ball handler. It tells the latter not only that the player is free for a pass but also, if correctly executed, where and when the player wishes to receive the ball. A signal may be executed with one or two hands, the fingers being extended and spread to give a large target.

A player should develop the habit, when on attack, of constantly signalling for the ball. The signal should be made to his side, away from the defender. When moving across court or towards the basket,

Pivot player (in black) uses a roll to create a passing lane

Player in black signals for the ball

a player should normally signal
with the leading hand, again if
possible, away from the defender.
The signal should lead the player
through on a cut to basket. The
pivot player, when moving away
from the basket towards the ball
handler, should try to signal with
both hands.

Passing

Basketball is a no contact game
and therefore possession of the
ball is crucial. Safe passing should
not always be equated with
effective passing, because although
an effective pass will be safe, a
safe pass may not be received in
the most advantageous position. To
be effective a pass must be taken
by the receiver **when** and **where**
he wants it and the importance of
both the timing of the pass and its
placing in relation to the position of
the receiver and the defender
should be stressed. It is a poor pass
if a player has moved and freed
himself and then does not receive
the ball until his defender has
recovered; equally, it is a poor
pass if a player, who is free,
receives the ball near his feet
rather than at the position from
where he can either pass to a
team-mate or take a shot. To help
players achieve this 'right time' and
'right place' an appreciation of the
following principles is necessary.

Safe passing

27

PRINCIPLES OF PASSING

Too often passing is considered solely from the point of view of the passer. The receiver has an important part to play in making the pass a success. We have already seen methods used to get free and the importance of signalling by the receiver. Before releasing the ball the passer must ensure that his team-mate is ready to receive.

Accuracy

The receiver needs to receive the ball at the right time and in the right place. A pass can be comfortably caught if received in front of the player—anywhere his hands can reach without making him bend or jump. If a team-mate is free and in a position for a shot, he wants the ball quickly and accurately so that he can start his shot immediately.

Speed of Pass

Having looked at the creation of space and direction of pass the next principle is that of time: the time taken by the ball to travel from passer to receiver. The more time taken by the pass, the more time opponents have to track the ball and to intercept. To cut down the opportunities for an interception most passes should be made aiming for the optimum speed; that is, the top speed for safe catching. Working on the premise that the shortest distance

between two points is a straight line, this means the use of a direct flight path from passer to receiver.

The fact that a slow pass takes time can be used to advantage by team-mates when passing. The passer may want to give a team-mate time to move to receive the ball, and so a pass may be lobbed to a player running down court on a fast break to give him time to move on to the ball.

Disguise Intentions

Although this will usually be thought of as the use of a fake or feint prior to passing, one of the most effective ways to disguise the intention is by using a fast release of the ball. The fast release depends upon good wrist and finger action and a minimum preparatory movement of the arms. This snap release of the ball takes time to develop. With beginners the coach should discourage excessive movements with the ball. Where movement is necessary it should be deliberate and purposeful.

It may be necessary to move the ball to protect it from an opponent. A pass may be started from various positions, either low or high; for example, the ball may be held low to make the opponent think that a low level pass is to be made and, as the opponent moves down, the pass is made over his shoulder. A player needs to

develop the use of peripheral vision to see the positions of opponents and team-mates.

Control of the Ball

Without ball control successful passing is a matter of luck. Obtaining maximum control requires two hands on the ball and contact being made with the fingers comfortably spread. The palm of the hand should be kept off the ball. Excessive movement of the ball for the purpose of faking frequently leads to some loss of control, which can prevent an immediate pass being possible. A passing opportunity may only occur for a fraction of a second and it is essential that the passer has the ball under sufficient control to make use of it immediately. Swinging the ball around, putting it behind the back or between the legs, means the passer must then waste time bringing it to a more favourable position before a pass can be made; these 'tricks' are usually non-effective from the attacking players' point of view.

An ability to read the game can, and must, be developed in all players. When passing the ball the player's first consideration should be to make a *safe* pass. The safe passing range is usually considered to be between $3\frac{1}{2}$–$4\frac{1}{2}$ metres (12–15 ft), unless a larger space is available which is free of opponents and into which the pass can be made. Signalling by team members provides a target, tells the ball handler that a player is ready to receive the ball and may help in deciding the direction and timing of the pass. The player passing the ball must still consider his own defender, who will be trying to prevent the pass: just because a team-mate signals, the ball handler does not have to pass —he must make the final decision as to whether it is possible to pass. When passing to a team-mate who is moving free, a player will need to develop the skill of passing to the space into which that player is heading. This involves awareness of team-mates' movements and the development of timing of passes so that the ball always arrives at a space just as the team-mate gets there.

IMPORTANCE OF THE PASSING LANE

Both the passer and potential receivers are concerned to open up passing lanes. The ball handler may change the position of the ball to establish a different passing lane; for example, instead of holding the ball at chest height it can be held above head height. This is a useful position for making passes over the head of a closely marking defender. Two other methods used by the ball handler to improve or create the passing lanes are to pivot or to dribble.

The dribble need only be one bounce so that a positional adjustment is made. The pivot can be used to alter the angle of the pass or to 'step through', that is, step close to and past a tightly marking defender.

The player with the ball should try to assess each situation as it develops, considering the following points:

☐ How far away is the team-mate: is he stationary or moving?

The chest pass

Remember the distance/time relationship—the longer distance passes give opponents more time to move in and intercept.

☐ How far away is the passer's opponent? If he is close, he will have less time to move his hands to intercept the pass; the further away he is, the more time he has for the interception.

☐ How closely marked is the potential pass receiver? If the team-mate is closely marked, the pass must be made on the side of the receiver, away from his defender.

☐ Can the pass requested by the team-mate's signal be made?

☐ Is an alternative pass possible and more productive to the team?

A skilled passer should try to be deceptive, and should disguise his intentions by looking well ahead and developing a solemn face. It is best not to stare at the receiver. The pass should be made quickly and firmly; quick release is preferable to fast, hard movement through the air.

The fast pass may involve a preparatory wind-up that will give the opponent a chance to anticipate the pass, and it may also be difficult for the team-mate to catch. Passes must be sympathetic. Whenever possible, passes should be in a horizontal plane.

The overhead pass

CHEST PASS

This pass is used when there is space, and speed is required. In the illustration on page 29 the pass is being used over short range.

OVERHEAD PASS

Guards and forwards should develop the use of the overhead pass—it is a quick alternative to a shot and is particularly valuable for short passing situations when players are closely marked, and for making a pass over smaller opponents. Pivot players should be expert in using this pass when unable to penetrate the defence and to take a shot. Against a pressing defence the pivot player has space to operate above head height, which may be difficult to defend. The use of an overhead pass to a pivot can help break a pressure defence. The illustration shows the overhead pass being used to pass the ball to a pivot player who has taken up a post position at the free-throw line.

BOUNCE PASS

The bounce pass should only be used when a safe horizontal pass is not possible. It is used in a close-passing situation or against a close-marking opponent, as illustrated, who has his arms up and may be bigger than the passer.

The bounce pass

OTHER PASSES

The majority of the passes so far considered are two-hand passes that will be used at the $3\frac{1}{2}$–$4\frac{1}{2}$ m (12–15 ft) range. A player's repertoire of passes increases as his game develops; these may be one- or two-handed. One-handed passes can be used to start a fast break, or be linked to a dribble when a player makes the pass one-handed without picking the ball up to end the dribble.

The development of passing ability will include making players aware of the play in front of them, of the relationship between the position of team-mates and opponents, and of the effect this has on passing. Passing needs to be linked with other skills, particularly footwork, so that players can handle the ball successfully when on the move (a natural running action should be

Overhead pass to a cutting player

stressed here). The dribble can be used to open up a passing lane; a one-bounce dribble can be used to alter a position so that a passing lane to a team-mate is created. Not all passes will be made to create the immediate scoring opportunity. They can be used to move the ball from one side of the court to the other; for example, the guard to guard pass. Another use is the pass out of a congested area for safety when an attacking play breaks down and to ensure possession is not lost so that a new attacking move can be started.

When passing to a cutting player (player moving to basket) the pass should be made ahead of him so that he can run on to it. The cutter does not want to have to check his movement; if he does, the defender he has beaten could well have time to recover.

RECEIVING A PASS

The receiver anticipates the receipt of the ball by signalling for the pass and concentrating on the ball to judge the flight path correctly. Although only one hand may be used to signal for the ball, two hands should be used for safe catching. As the ball is received the player should reach out to meet the ball early, allowing 'give' in the hands to help absorb the force of the pass. It may be necessary to catch and protect the ball; if so, the ball is held firmly but turned, so

that one hand is above it and one below. The arms and hands will then protect the ball from an underhand slap. This also enables the ball to be pressed firmly into the shooting hand. It is not pulled close to the body—in this position it is difficult to make a quick pass and is easier for an opponent to tie up the ball handler and gain a held ball.

CREATING THE SPACE FOR THE SHOOTING CHANCE

Once the pass is received the player should pivot immediately to look for the basket. If, on pivoting,

the player finds that he is within scoring range and has sufficient time and space, a shot should be taken. This pivot to face the basket creates a 'triple threat' situation. The player can shoot, drive (dribble to basket) or pass. Looking at the basket also identifies any team-mates who are close to it and available to receive a pass. Having received the ball within shooting range, if a shot is not immediately possible because of a close marking defender, the player should attempt to create space for the shot. Space may be found at the side or in front of the defender.

Receiving a pass in two hands

The illustration shows a player who has come to a jump stop and is threatening to shoot. As the defender moves to cover the shot the attacking player steps past him to shoot.

Once the player has pivoted to face the basket, and the defender is not in line between it and the attacker but is still close, a drive forwards for a closer shot should be made. This one versus one attacking play using the dribble is covered on page 44.

Another method of creating space for the shot is to jump and shoot. Timing is obviously important and a fake may be necessary before a player goes up for the shot. The fake is used to place the defender off balance so he cannot interfere with the shot. The illustration shows the attacking player stepping away from the opponent and 'fading' slightly to create space for the shot. This requires a high level of shooting skill, as the fade places the shooter slightly off balance.

A player who receives the ball when close to the basket, but finds that the defender has a position between him and the basket, can create space for the shot by stepping past the defender, or by faking a move in one direction and then stepping towards the goal through the gap so created.

Stepping 'through' for a shot after a jump shot

Player in black jumps to create space for the shot

SHOOTING

Having created space for a shot, it is essential to be able to score consistently. It has already been established that it is vital to look for a shot early. However, because the target is an empty space it is important to select a point as near to that space as possible. When making an 'off the board' shot, commonly used for lay-up and hook shots, the player should focus on a spot within or near to the rectangle above the basket. In other shots he may select a point on the rim; personal preference will help the player to choose whether this is the front or rear edge, and once it has been decided the aim should be at the same place during practice so that it becomes habitual.

Regular practice is essential to obtain accuracy in shooting. Since most practice will not take place in the presence of the coach, it is important for players to understand some of the principles which will affect the accuracy of their shots.

To develop a high level of concentration, practise shooting under conditions as near as possible to those found in the game. The ritual seen as a player prepares to take a free shot, the adjustment of the feet and bouncing of the ball, is an attempt to stimulate relaxation and confidence, the foundations for which have been laid during practice. During the game it is necessary to shoot under conditions of physical and mental stress. The opponents will constantly be trying to distract the shooter and discourage him from taking an accurate shot. Therefore, part of shooting practice should be against an opponent; the adjustments necessary to counter defensive moves will help to improve timing and develop speed of shot, which are so important if the player is to be able to take advantage of defensive errors.

The lay up shot

During practice the player should concentrate on the following:

☐ Looking for the shot early, concentrating on the rim before, during, and after the shot, at least until the shot has scored or missed.

☐ Holding the ball firmly in both hands, with fingers spread.

☐ Shooting with one hand. The wrist of the shooting hand should be cocked back before the shot; the non-shooting hand steadies the ball.

☐ Shooting with a strong wrist and finger flick; the follow-through with the wrist will then give a natural back-spin to the ball as it leaves the fingers.

☐ The elbow of the shooting arm should be nearly under the ball so that the straightening of the arm directs the ball towards the basket.

☐ Being on balance and under control during the shot. This promotes a smooth follow-through, which is essential for accuracy. Balance starts at the feet, so always establish a firm foot position before shooting.

The shot to be used will largely depend on how the player has created or made use of space. The basic shots are illustrated, with comments on each shooting action. As players develop their game they establish their own style of shooting, based upon these basic shooting actions. At the end of a dribble, having escaped from the defender, a player would normally use a lay-up shot if close to the basket.

LAY-UP SHOT

This shot should be mastered by all players, as it forms the basis from which different shooting styles can be developed for close-to-basket shots. The essential ingredients of the shot are that it is taken on the move, usually on the run, the player jumps up and towards the basket as he shoots, and stretches to release the ball as close to the basket as possible. In the illustration the player moving forwards has picked the ball up at the end of a dribble (or after receiving a pass); the ball is firmly held in both hands and the head is lifted, as the ball is gathered, to look for the basket early. The illustrations show the ball being taken by a player landing first on his right foot, and then on his left foot as he makes a long final step. This enables him to control his forward momentum and helps him to prepare for the high jump off the left foot. As he jumps off one foot, he carries the ball upwards, still in both hands. Notice that the take-off foot for the shot is on the opposite side to the shooting hand. The player releases the ball at full stretch from one hand, using the backboard to deflect it into the basket.

SET SHOT

This shot in the modern game is used for distance shots should the defender 'sag off'. It is the shot that many players use when attempting the three-point scoring shot. It is sometimes used when shooting over a front screen, but is most commonly made when a player is taking a free throw. The illustration shows a player using a set shot from the free-throw line. Notice that he takes up a stride position with his feet, the forward foot being on the same side as his shooting hand. Prior to taking the shot he bends his knees slightly. If he were taking this shot during the normal course of play he would be

The set shot

using a basic attacking stance that involves a similar position with the feet and a slight flexion of the knees. The player looks at the basket throughout the shot. He follows through with a vigorous snap of the wrist and fingers and, with the powerful drive from the legs, finishes the shot at full stretch.

JUMP SHOT

This is perhaps the most effective shot in the modern game. When used in conjunction with a fake it is a very difficult shot to defend, unless the opponent has a considerable height advantage. The shot may be from a stationary position following a head or foot

fake, after a pivot, after receiving a pass, or at the end of a dribble. When developing the jump shot the player must learn to take it following a jump stop and from a stride stop at the end of a dribble.

The player takes off from both feet and jumps vertically, attempting to release the ball when in an almost stationary position near the top of the jump. The timing of the jump should enable him to avoid defensive attempts to intercept the shot. The timing of the shot during the jump is also important.

The illustration shows a player taking a jump shot. He jumps from two feet, taking the ball up in front of his face to be held above his forehead. Then he concentrates on the basket and, near the top of his jump, releases the ball with an upward extension of the arms, flipping the ball towards the basket with a vigorous wrist and finger action. Notice the carriage of the ball in two hands, with the shooting hand behind the ball.

DUNK SHOT

This is a shot in which a jumping player puts the ball down into the opponent's basket from above. The shot should be thought of as a development of the lay-up shot; instead of jumping high to place the ball on the backboard, in the dunk the player aims to place the ball down into the basket. To do this he needs to be able to jump and carry the ball in one or two hands above the level of the ring, i.e. to a height of 10 feet.

Too often this shot is considered to be one which only players of nearly 7 feet in height should attempt, but any reasonably athletic player about 6 feet tall should believe himself capable of dunking.

In the dunk the player aims to drop the ball softly down into the basket. Leg strength and agility, together with ability to time the

The jump shot

The dunk shot

38

jump and reach, are important to enable maximum height to be gained. Dunking requires positive thinking by players and their coaches.

HOOK SHOT

This shot is used when the player is close to the basket and is particularly valuable when the ball is received by a player who has his back to the basket. Having received the ball, the player will glance over his shoulder to establish where his opponent is stationed. He then steps away, looking early for the basket and continuing to hold the ball firmly in both hands. The step is made onto the foot which is on the opposite side to the shooting hand. The player jumps off this foot, reaching and stretching for the shot, which is completed with a flick of the wrist and fingers. When he turns, the player looks at the target and concentrates on it throughout the shot. The follow-through he makes after the shot brings him into a good position, facing the basket, to move for a rebound.

Players should practise taking the hook shot with either hand, as it makes them more difficult to defend. This shot will also be used by a player moving to basket either with a step shown in the illustration or at the end of a drive. The player moving to basket finds that the opponent has allowed him to come in close but has prevented a clear lay-up shot. In such a situation the player would use the footwork of the lay-up shot, but instead of taking the ball up in front of his face he would take it up to the side, away from the opponent, and would use a hook shot action to shoot the ball softly over the opponent's head towards the target. This hook lay-up shot may involve the player moving slightly away from the target as he shoots, something that is not

A hook shot used in a game situation

39

encouraged with novices. However, as beginners develop their game and gain greater control over their shooting they should consider developing a jump shot in which they fade away from their opponents slightly, thus creating space for the shot. In the hook shot the player uses his body to protect the shooting arm from the defender.

POWER SHOTS

In addition to the hook shot, which helps develop close-to-basket play, players need to become proficient at power shots. A power shot taken by a player close to the basket can be considered a cross

Excellent execution of the hook shot

Power shot following a rebound

between a lay-up shot and a jump shot, and will involve stepping to basket as mentioned earlier under the heading of 'creating space for a shot'.

The illustration on page 41 shows how, following a rebound, the attacking player finds that the defender has allowed him space under the basket. He steps and jumps through the space created to lay the ball against the backboard, and scores. This shot has the advantage that should the player be fouled and prevented from scoring he will be awarded two free throws, because he is in his shooting action from the moment he moves. If he were to dribble through the space and be fouled while doing so, his team would only be awarded the ball at the side line, since a player is not in the act of shooting until he has picked the ball up from the dribble. Players also make use of a power shot at the end of a fast dribble to basket when either the defender has left some space, but insufficient for a straight lay-up shot, or the attacking player's footwork is wrong for a straight lay-up, so he lands on two feet simultaneously and changes his forward movement into an upward lift towards the backboard.

THE DRIBBLE

It is essential to learn to dribble if a player is to realise his potential.

Since the dribble enables a player to move with the ball, it increases his mobility when on the attack. This should not be wasted by aimlessly bouncing the ball.

Remember that before a dribble a player is 'alive' and may move anywhere, but after the dribble he is 'dead' and may not dribble again. Before using the dribble the player is a triple threat, being able to pass, shoot or dribble, and this creates problems for the defender. After dribbling the player may pass or shoot, but he has lost the option of moving with the ball and is therefore easier to defend.

Players should try to master the following skills to improve overall dribbling ability:

☐ Control the ball by spreading the fingers comfortably, so that they contact as much of the ball as possible.

☐ Push the ball down firmly using hand, elbow and wrist.

☐ The hand should be on top of the ball. This will prevent 'palming' and ensure that the ball rebounds back to the hand accurately.

☐ The head should be held up so that the player can see team-mates and opponents.

☐ The force of the ball as it rebounds from the floor should be absorbed by the fingers, wrist and arm. The ball should not be batted or slapped.

☐ Players should be able to dribble with either hand.

☐ Players should be able to stop at the end of a dribble without travelling or charging into an opponent and committing a foul.

☐ Players should be able to change direction and speed, and to stop and start quickly.

☐ Players should be able to avoid being double teamed by opponents.

☐ Eliminate the use of the single bounce dribble. It will reduce your effectiveness as an attacker.

The Dribble as a Weapon in Attack

The dribble is used extensively by a guard when bringing the ball up the court. When there is no opposition, he should bounce the ball high in front of his body; this enables him to concentrate on the situation ahead. His approach may be fast or slow, and he should look for opportunities to pass or shoot.

When challenged by a defender, it may be necessary to protect the ball. The knees should be bent, the dribble lowered and the ball brought to the side of the body. The non-dribbling arm and foot are used to give additional protection.

An attacker may dribble into a space near the basket and, as defenders move to adjust their defensive positions to cover the threat, he may leave a space into which a team-mate can move, signal and receive a pass. Defenders will frequently overplay the dribbling hand and attackers can make use of this fact to create a passing lane to a team-mate.

Although speed of dribble is important, it must be controlled during a fast break. An attacking player should use a high dribble, so that he can adopt a normal running posture, and should make a pumping action of the arms so that the ball rebounds in front of his body.

When attackers find themselves playing against a man-to-man full court pressing defence, a useful way to beat it is to give the ball to the best dribbler and to get out of his way so that he can bring the ball down court against one defender.

INDIVIDUAL ATTACK WITH THE BALL

The player with the ball can take a shot, dribble the ball, pass to a team-mate, or hold the ball. Before he chooses one of these options he may fake, but the decision will be influenced by the opposition. Prior to receiving the ball the player may have been forced by a close-marking opponent to move and free himself to receive the pass. The player who is holding the ball, but not facing the basket, is not a direct threat to the defenders unless he is close to the backboard.

To threaten the opposition the player must pivot to face the basket once the ball has been controlled.

PROTECTION OF THE BALL

Initially this will involve two hands on the ball and, after catching, bringing it in close to the body. It may be insufficient and a pivot by the attacking player to move away from the defender may be necessary, but the player should still try to maintain a position facing the basket. Additional protection can be given by placing the ball in such a way that the body shields it from the defender, and in extreme cases a player may even pivot so that he has his back

Protection of the ball on the dribble

43

to the basket and opponent. In this instance he has lost his quick shot option and is protecting the ball so well that he has done the job of the opponent by defending the basket from the ball! The ball can also be protected by holding it high, which is particularly useful for tall players. However, it should be noted that in this position the player limits his choices. With the ball up he will be slower to start a dribble, because the distance the ball has to travel to the floor has been increased. On the other hand, it is a useful position for passing the ball over the head of a defender to a team-mate in the under-basket area. In protecting the ball the player should endeavour to maintain a position that threatens the opposition and also disguises his intentions.

ATTACKING OPTIONS

With a number of options from which to choose it will be of help to the inexperienced player if he develops a routine for considering the possibilities. The options and the order in which they should be thought about is as follows:

☐ look to pass to a team-mate close to the basket; if there is no team-mate free, then

☐ look to shoot; if that is not an option, then

☐ look to dribble to a new position (in particular use a drive closer to the basket and a possible shot); if that is not possible, then

☐ look to pass to a team-mate. Of course, once the player has passed the ball he still has one final offensive option and that is

☐ to move to a new position.

Simplified, the attacking options are *look to pass under, or shoot, or drive, or pass, or move.*

The player is protecting the ball by holding it high above his head

SHOOTING OPTION

The player's shooting option decision will take into account his skill, distance from the basket and the position of the defenders. Players should aim to develop an ability to score a high percentage of shots from the $4\frac{1}{2}$ m (15 feet) plus range. If a player is a scoring threat from this distance, he will force a defender to take up a closer position to him. It is important for individuals to learn to relate their own shooting skills to the position of opponents. The closer the defender, the more difficult it is to score consistently; and it is consistency in shooting that wins games. This will come with ability in shot selection. In the game situation the player needs to:

☐ recognise how near the basket he needs to be to have a good chance of scoring;

☐ recognise when he is clear of a defender and able to shoot.

DRIBBLE OPTION

The dribble is used in the present attacking context to move the player who has the ball to a new position, usually closer to the basket for a higher percentage shot. The rules limit a player to one dribble, and players have to learn when this is most effective. Initially we can consider use of the dribble in the attacking situation, when the player with the ball endeavours to

get past a defender standing between himself and the basket. In this one-versus-one situation, the dribble past an opponent is an important attacking weapon. The dribble straight to basket is called a drive.

The attacking player with the ball will be looking for errors by the defender. If, for example, the player with the ball faces the basket and finds no defender between himself and the goal, he should drive straight in to take a

Drive for goal!

closer shot. Other defensive mistakes will arise from the defender's incorrect balance.

Since the defender's balance depends upon his stance, and in particular his foot position, a player should attack a defender who takes a defensive position with one foot clearly in front of the other. If a defender has taken a defensive stance with his right foot well forward, the dribbler should attack his foot and dribble to the defender's right.

With attacking and defensive players starting from an almost stationary position the mistakes in balance, relative to the attacker and the basket, that the defender can make are:

Moving towards attacking opponents

This is the mistake most commonly made by defenders who, after the man they are marking has received a pass, rush towards him. In such a situation they can be easily caught off balance and beaten.

Upward movement by the defender

Should the opponent jump to defend an anticipated shot there will be space to drive past him for the basket. While the defender is going up, the attacking player dribbles around him. For the attacking player the fake to shoot may need to be no more than looking at the basket and lifting the ball and shoulders slightly. This move is occasionally called 'up and under'.

Backward movement by the defender

If the attacker fakes to drive by stepping towards the basket, then as the defender moves backwards to cover the attacker can pivot back away from him and shoot. The movement is sometimes called a 'rocker step'. The illustration on pages 48 and 49 shows player number 6 using this fake to move the defender backwards. Obviously, as the attacking player pivots back to take the shot the defender may move forwards to cover, leaving an opportunity for the attacking player to drive for basket past an incoming defender.

The player in white drives past when the defender moves forwards

The fake shot and the drive

46

Sideways Movement by the Defender

Provided an attacker has not used his dribble, he may force the defender into making the mistake of moving sideways in response to a fake step before the dribble. In the illustration on pages 48 and 49 the defender has made two errors: firstly he has moved towards the attacking opponent and, secondly, he has fallen for a fake to the side. The attacking player pretends to start his dribble to the left by making a jab step in that direction; as the defender shifts to cover, the attacker steps again with his left foot across his opponent, driving to basket with his right hand. Throughout the fake step the player uses his right foot as his pivot foot. When using this move, the player should remember that the rules say that the pivot foot must remain grounded until the ball is released at the start of the dribble. If the defensive movement is to the attacker's left, the dribble is made to the right, and vice versa.

To cause the defenders to make one of these mistakes a fake may be necessary. If a fake that involves movement by the attacking player is used, it should not put the attacker off balance. Remember that upon receiving the ball close to the basket a player should always look for his shot before considering a dribble. It will also help him to assess his defender's position. Normally the latter will be positioned between the attacker and the basket, preventing a straight drive to goal. There is now a 'cat and mouse' situation. Can the defender be moved away from this position to create space for a drive? With the fake the attacker will try to make the defender move forwards, upwards, sideways or backwards and thus force him into a defensive error of judgment.

Top photographs *The rocker step*

Bottom photographs *The step fake followed by the drive*

Dribble incorporating change of direction

The reverse dribble

OTHER ATTACKING MOVES USING THE DRIBBLE

In those attacking moves already described which utilise the dribble the player has started from a stationary position. The dribbler should also be capable of beating an opponent when both are moving. For example, when the dribbler takes the ball towards the basket the defender may cover this move. It may be possible to beat him by a quick change of direction of the dribble, taking advantage of space on his other side.

The illustration (top) shows a player dribbling to his right; as the defender adjusts his position to cover the move, the attacking player takes the ball to the left in front of his body, at the same time driving hard off the right foot to change his direction and take advantage of space created on the other side of the defender.

REVERSE DRIBBLE

Another method of beating an opponent who overplays the dribbling hand is to use a reverse dribble. This move is similar to the 'change hands and change direction', except that as the illustration shows the dribbler pivots and turns his back on his opponent, thus rolling round and past the defender. The move should be used when the defensive player is too close for the attacker to switch dribbling hands across and in front of his body. For example, when dribbling with the right hand to the left-hand side of the defender and the latter adjusts to cover, the dribbler should check his movement and execute a stride stop. As he pivots on his front foot, he should change his dribbling hand, rolling with his back to the defender and completing the drive to the defender's right. As the dribbler rolls, it is important that he takes a long step past the opponent.

When bringing the ball down court against a close-marking defender a guard may use a number of reverses to force the defender to retreat. This movement is sometimes

51

referred to as backing the defender up, and the dribbler will use a side-stepping shuffle, changing hands to protect the ball.

A variation of the reverse dribble is the spin dribble. In this action, however, when the ball is brought back to reverse the direction, it is dragged round with the hand that was used initially. The player only switches the dribbling hand when the new direction is chosen and he can drive past the defender. The disadvantage of the reverse dribble (and spin) is that the dribbler loses sight momentarily of team-mates and defender.

CHANGE OF SPEED AND RHYTHM

During any dribble sequence changes of speed and rhythm may be sufficient to give the dribbler the half-pace advantage necessary to get him free. Good footwork is essential during the dribble, as it enables the player to stop and change direction while maintaining good balance. A player should learn to stop at the end of a dribble using either a stride or a jump stop. After the forward movement is halted the player may pivot to protect the ball or to make space for a shot or pass. A useful dribbling move to develop is one in which the initial movement is made at a single speed. The defender's reaction to this will be to retreat.

The dribbler then executes a stop, but keeps the dribble going; as the defender checks his backward movement and adjusts to move closer, the dribbler tries to accelerate past him. This hesitation dribble is a useful addition to a player's skills.

DRIBBLER CREATING A SCREEN FOR A TEAM-MATE

When a dribbler's forward progress is blocked by a defender a quick stop and pivot away from the defender may create a screen situation for a team-mate to utilise. In the illustration a team-mate uses the screen for a jump shot. If the team-mate who uses the dribbler as a screen had been closely marked, he could have moved in such a way as to 'brush' the defender off on the dribbler who has been forced to stop.

USING A DRIBBLE TO MANOEUVRE AN OPPONENT INTO A SCREEN

A player may use a screen to help him lose a close-marking opponent. The word 'screen' is used to express the legal means of obstructing the movement of an opponent. The dribbler backs the defender up to the screen, using a shuffling action with the feet; he then reverses, pivoting close to the team-mate who has established the screen. The dribbler moves free for a shot or drive to basket.

INDIVIDUAL OFFENCE WITHOUT THE BALL

With only one player able to have the ball in his possession at any one time, a player has to learn to play for the major part of the game without the ball. A player without the ball needs to be alert to what

Creating a screen

is happening on court and he needs to curb his desire to move constantly to a new position to receive the pass.

MOVING FREE TO RECEIVE A RETURN PASS

Moving to receive a pass will include changes of direction and speed to beat the close-marking defender.

The attacking player, having passed the ball, should seek opportunities to move to receive a return pass. This may involve looking for defender errors, errors similar to those already covered under 'Dribbling', that is, mistakes in position and/or balance. The defender who is marking the passer may move to intercept the pass or watch to see where the ball has gone. Both these actions are errors which the player without

the ball should attack by cutting (moving without the ball) towards the basket and looking for a return pass.

ESTABLISHING A POSITION AS A SCREEN

An attacking player can take up a position which obstructs the path of a defender who is endeavouring to maintain his correct defensive position between man and basket. When the screen is set along his path, the defender is forced to change direction and generally check his movement, and this gives an attacking player an advantage of time and space that can lead to a scoring opportunity. The attacking player may stand to the side of, in front of, or behind a stationary defender when setting a screen, but if set behind the defender, it must be at least one

metre from him. Both front and side screens may be set at any distance from an opponent, short of actual contact. The player establishing the screen can face in any direction, and if he sets it on an opponent who is moving he should position himself about one to two metres from the defender. The distance depends on the latter's speed of movement.

INDIVIDUAL DEFENCE

Individual defence based upon sound man-to-man principles is essential for good team defence.

A player's responsibilities in defence against an individual opponent may be listed as follows:

☐ Discourage opponent from shooting from a high percentage scoring area.

☐ Anticipate his moves to

discourage him from driving past and getting closer to the basket for a shot.

☐ Make it difficult for him to pass accurately, particularly into the high percentage scoring area.

☐ Discourage the attacker from running past to receive a pass and prevent him from collecting a rebound.

☐ Make it difficult for him to receive a pass, especially in the high percentage scoring area.

☐ Perform the above without committing a foul.

Defensive Position

Initially the defensive position will be 'in line' between the opponent and the basket. If the opponent is within shooting range, the defender should be close enough to discourage the shot. Should the opponent be away from the ball, the defender can 'sag off' him towards the basket he is defending, changing his stance so he can see the opponent and the ball.

Defensive Stance and Footwork

The basic defensive position mentioned earlier is not static, or the opponent will be able to move past. To prevent penetration by a cutting or driving player, the defender will need to react and move backwards quickly. Good individual defence is based upon the use of the feet; the stance is the basic basketball stance which will facilitate movement. This is a low position: feet are spread about shoulder width apart, with the toe of one foot in line with the heel of the other foot, knees are bent and hips are slightly flexed. The forward foot will usually be the inside foot, that is, the one nearer the centre of the court. The basic defensive stance has been described as the 'toilet position'. To match movements by the opponent the defender uses a short step and drag action with the feet, keeping the knees apart and not crossing the feet. Should it be necessary to run to regain a defensive position against an opponent, the player should use a normal sprinting action.

The basic stance is maintained when moving forwards towards an opponent, perhaps in an attempt to discourage a shot. In this situation there is a danger of moving too quickly. Remember the attacking options, and that the closer the defender is to the attacker the less time there will be to react to his movements. The defender aims to retain a low position and to keep contact with the floor, as this will enable changes in direction to be made quickly. Before a dribble an opponent with the ball is 'alive', so the defender needs to be especially alert. If the opponent is within his shooting range, then the forward hand will be up to discourage the shot. If the defender has his right foot forwards and the attacker tries to penetrate with a right-hand dribble to the defender's left, then the defender should drop his left foot back to cover the penetration, continuing to shuffle by leading with the left foot as shown in the illustration. (Notice a hand is down to force the dribbler to protect the ball.)

Should the dribbler go to the right of the defender, the first foot movement is a step back with the right foot and then the shuffle to cover the dribble.

Defending the dribbler

USE OF THE ARMS AND HANDS

The arms should be flexed and the hands carried at about shoulder height, with the palms of the hands facing the ball. The arms are flexed to enable quick movement to be made in any direction. When playing against a dribbler the defender should keep his hands low, so that should the dribbler make an error and fail to protect the ball with his body he can seize upon the chance to steal the ball. This should be done with an upward movement of the hands. Using the hands in such a manner is less likely to result in a foul or to move the defender off balance. Quick hands and vigorous movements of the arms are essential to good defence. The 'windmill' action of the arms may be used effectively to discourage an accurate pass, especially in an out-of-bounds situation.

The hands are particularly valuable for feeling for screens when a player is moving backwards. The arms and hands are used to bluff, bother, disconcert or distract attacking efforts to shoot, drive or pass. The hands should be thought of, and used, as dissuaders. Dissuade the opponent from shooting and dribbling or passing in his chosen direction. The hands play an important part in defensive efforts to pressure the passing lane.

DEFENDING AGAINST A DRIBBLER

A player is able to change direction quickly by the use of a bent knee stance and a shuffling action with the feet to cover movement by the dribbler.

Defending against a dribbler should not be considered simply a matter of following the dribbler. A defender can pressure the attacker by adjusting his position so that the dribbling hand is overplayed. This can be particularly effective against a dribbler who is very weak on one hand, usually the left. In this case the defender moves from the basic 'in-line' position over to the side of the strong hand. For the right-hand dribbler the defender moves slightly to his left, so that his nose is in line with the dribbler's arm. To keep the ball protected the dribbler must now use either the weak left hand or try to go the longer way round the defender using the right-hand dribble. Both these movements are to the defender's advantage. Alternatively, the defender could allow the dribbler to use his strong hand but, by exaggerating his defensive stance, channel the dribbler in the direction of the strong hand. In the illustration the defender has taken a position to channel the dribbler to his right hand.

Should the opponent gain an advantage the defender will break from the shuffle step and run at full speed to regain the defensive position between the opponent and the basket. The defender heads towards the basket to be defended, as attacking players frequently go on a curve to basket.

After a dribble the attacker is 'dead' and the defender should learn to react quickly to the situation. If he is within shooting range the defender moves in to a close range, with both hands up to prevent the shot. The defender is safe in taking this close position because the attacking player cannot dribble. The defender should adopt a stance with feet wide spread to discourage the attacker from stepping past for a shot. If the opponent is outside shooting range, the defender can either sag off and attempt to intercept his pass or move in close to pressure him into an error or tying the ball up; through good use of the hands he can obtain a 5 seconds' violation by the opponent. Which option is used will depend upon the player's assessment of the opponent and the defence tactics the coach has given. The illustration shows a double team on the player with the ball and 'fronting' the post player to deny reception.

Steering the dribbler

Double-teaming the ball handler and fronting the post player

DEFENCE OFF THE BALL

When a player is marking away from the ball adjustments to the in-line principle may be necessary, so that he can see his opponent and the ball. A strict in-line defence may leave spaces in the defence near the ball. By slightly adjusting to an off-line position, it may be possible for a team to cover potential scoring areas. If the opponent is one pass away then the defensive tactic could be a pass denial. This should always occur when the opponents are in the under-basket or in a high percentage scoring area. Notice in the illustration of pass denial that the foot and arm closest to the ball handler are forward, with the arm in the passing lane. The defender is looking down his arm to see both ball handler and his opponent, and moving, as the opponent moves, to deny pass reception.

The further the opponent is from the ball, the further the defender will be from his opponent and the closer he will be to the basket he is defending. When defending against an opponent who is away from the ball the defender establishes a triangle of ball-defender-opponent, as in the diagram.

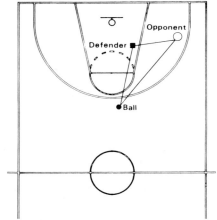

Figure 5 *Ball-defender opponent triangle*

The defender should be alert to his opponent cutting into the key and to the pass. Since the defender is closer to the ball than his opponent, he should be able to react and cover any cut towards the ball by the opponent.

If the pivot moves to a high position, then the defender will usually take a position behind, although he could adjust to deny pass reception.

With the pivot player taking up a position half-way down the lane the coach is likely to want him defended to prevent pass reception. This could involve fronting the pivot, or the defender could take a position to the side of him, with a hand in the passing lane. In the latter case the defender will be on the baseline side of the pivot, with his feet straddling the attacking player's foot that is nearest the baseline. If the pivot player receives the ball, he must turn towards the middle of the lane where the defender should have help.

THINKING ON DEFENCE

Good individual defence is played with the two 'ends' of the body, the feet and the brain. The feet are used to maintain a defensive position while the brain works out what the attacking opponent may do. Once the player has brought his brain into action to help him defend he can use his hands and arms advantageously. If he has heart and is prepared to take pride in his defensive ability, he will be a very useful member of any basketball team.

A player should try to analyse the

Defending to deny a pass reception

opponent's moves, his strengths and weaknesses:

☐ Is he a good dribbler; can he use either hand?

☐ Does he shoot; what is his range?

☐ When he drives does he always go the same way?

☐ Does he bounce the ball before every shot?

☐ Does he signal and move to free himself for a shot?

☐ Does he use the same fake every time?

☐ Does he react to a defensive fake?

☐ If you fake to steal the ball will he stop his dribble?

☐ What is his role in the attacking team?

Answers to these questions should enable the player to anticipate possible moves and help him to reduce his opponent's potential as an attacking player. Re-read the list of possible mistakes by defenders and remember that as a defender the player should aim not to make these mistakes. Don't rush forward, don't jump up; when a player sets off to dribble past don't move laterally, but step back; don't move too far away from an opponent who is a capable shooter.

BLOCKING OUT AND REBOUNDING

Blocking out is the gaining of an advantageous position between opponent and the backboard when a shot is taken. From this position a player should be able to jump and catch the rebound of the missed shot. The defender who has started from an inside defensive position starts with an advantage, but he must work to maintain this advantage. The two illustrations show player number 11 blocking-out his opponent, in the first instance when the opponent has shot and in the second when the opponent's team-mate has shot

Blocking out the shooter

the ball. Notice that the player blocking out in both instances has concentrated on the opponent and has pivoted into the path that the attacking player wishes to take to move to the basket. The player has established a strong blocking-out position with the attacker on his back. This strong position enables the defender to resist contact; if he did not, he would be liable to be pushed underneath the basket into a bad rebounding position. The player blocking out has his knees bent and feet wide apart; his elbows are out and his arms are carried at shoulder height, or below, so they can be used to help lift him up for the rebound.

Having blocked out, the defender should now be in a position from which he can time his jump and go for the rebound. When going for the rebound he reaches up for the ball with both hands, trying to time his jump so that he catches the ball at full stretch. Inexperienced players frequently jump too early for a rebound and find they have landed again before the ball reaches them. They should learn to time the jump and are advised not to go up for the rebound until they see the ball leave the backboard or ring.

REBOUNDING IN ATTACK

An attacking player will find it more difficult to obtain the inside position in a rebound situation. He should look for the defender turning to watch the ball as the shot goes up, and then cut into the gap under the basket. To prevent himself being blocked out, he could try using a feint to help create space for a rebound. If he

Blocking out and rebounding non-shooter

obtained a position in front of the backboard, with knees bent, close enough to be able to make a vertical jump for the ball, he would be less likely to foul. To time his jump the ball should be watched closely.

Tall attacking players and good jumpers may be able to tip the missed shot back into the basket. In the tip shot the ball should be cushioned momentarily on the fingers (so the player gains control) before being flicked towards the basket. Should an attacking player catch the rebound and

not be able to tip the ball, he should immediately look for an

opportunity to go straight back up for a shot.

Fight for the rebound!

The offensive rebound and shot

CO-OPERATIVE SKILLS

Although a basketball team consists of five players on court, it is usually through the efforts of two and occasionally three team-mates combining that one player is freed for a shot. This does not imply that players who are not involved have no task—they must keep the defender occupied so that he cannot help cover the attacker who is free. The game of basketball changes rapidly: one moment a player will find himself creating space for a team-mate and the next trying to work with a team-mate to free another for a shot. Two-versus-two and three-versus-three plays are the basic team skills that players need to develop. These become the building blocks for team play. In describing them coverage of both attacking and defensive play is included under each heading.

GIVE AND GO

Attack

In this play the players do just as the title suggests—*give* the ball to a team-mate and then *go* to the basket, looking for a return pass.

Any two players on court can work together in this way, with one taking advantage of a mistake by his opponent to cut free, or make a move (for example, a change of direction) to beat him. In the same way this play is commonly used by a guard and a forward. The guard passes ahead to the forward and then cuts for basket, looking for the return pass. When playing against an inexperienced defender the guard may find that, as the pass is made ahead to the forward, the defender will be tempted to turn to see where the ball has gone. At such a moment the guard is free and should immediately cut for basket, signalling for the return pass. Even though the opponent may not turn his head, he may still move off balance in an attempt to intercept the pass. If the defender does not make an unforced error, the attacking player may actually force an error through using a change of direction and pace to cut to basket. The photographs

show the guard, after passing initially, moving to his left, changing direction to his right by driving hard off his left foot, and cutting to basket for the return pass.

Defence

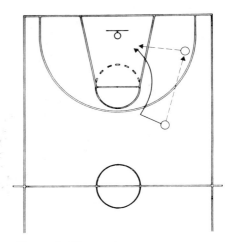

Figure 6 *Give and go*

For the defensive team the potentially dangerous situation is just after the ball has been passed. Obviously the defender will endeavour not to make the

A post play attack

mistakes mentioned earlier. When the pass is made, the defender marking the player who has passed should immediately sag back, that is, move back towards the basket. This gives the defender more time in which to cover any cut. Having made the step away from the opponent the defender changes his stance so that he can see both the ball and the man he is marking. It helps if the defender can point one arm at the ball and the other at the opponent. If the defender is playing well, he will find that every time the attacking team passes or moves the ball on a dribble the defender will move and adjust his defensive position.

POST PLAY
Attack
One of the basic screen situations that can be used in the game is a variation on the 'give and go'. The attacking player passes ahead and cuts to basket, looking for the return pass, but instead of cutting and keeping space between himself and the ball handler, as in the give and go, he cuts close to his team-mate. This causes the defender marking the cutter to check his movement momentarily, due to the position on court of the attacker's team-mate.

Such action should free the cutter for a return pass. This type of screen situation is called a 'post play'. In the post play illustrated the pivot player moves out from the under-basket area to receive a pass at the free-throw line. Here the pivot player will use a jump stop in taking the ball and landing. The guard, after making the pass, cuts close to the pivot player, who pivots to turn his back on the opponent marking the cutter. The guard is now free, and receives a pass and moves in for a shot before the defenders have had time to recover.

This basic post play action can be

Defending post play—going over the top

used from a number of different angles to the basket. A useful guide to its operation is that the player setting the post should attempt to take up a position along a straight line between the team-mate about to use the post and the basket. It does not have to be a pivot player who sets a post, it will frequently be a forward who creates a post situation for use by a team-mate. The attacking player who is about to cut past the post should, after passing, move away from the direction of the cut, then change direction and cut past the post. This makes the task of the defending player more difficult. The player creating the post can pivot into the path of the defender, but the rules require that the opponent should be given a space of between one and two metres in

which to stop and change direction. This pivot by the player setting the post enables him to face the basket and see the under-basket area of the court. The pivot player moving out from the under-basket area to receive the pass is moving towards the ball, which is a basic principle of pass reception. Through making this movement the pass is easier for the passer and it is more difficult to intercept by the defenders. The pass used will frequently be an overhead pass or a bounce pass.

Defence
The defence to this move is for the player making the initial pass to step back away from his opponent immediately the pass is made. This gives the defender more time to cover the cut. If the defender marking the post player warns his

team-mate that a post has been set, it will help prevent the screen situation being successful. The defender should endeavour to follow the cutter and go over the top of the post.

The defence should aim to deny passes into the player setting the post. If the screen is successful and the cutter receives an early return pass, his progress may be delayed by the post player's defender stepping out to take a charge or force the cutter wide (as in the illustration on page 66). He may even switch to take the cutter. However, normally a delay, a 'headging-out' tactic, is employed, as switching enables the post player to move closer to the basket for a return pass and therefore an easier shot.

BACKDOOR

Attack
Another method of beating an opponent is to use a backdoor cut. It can be employed when the opponent overplays the passing lane to prevent a pass being made. When this occurs the player being overplayed should fake to move out to receive the ball, then reverse direction and move at speed towards the basket, signalling for the ball. It is not as simple as give and go, as the player cutting to basket could have two defenders between himself and the ball handler, and the team-mate holding the ball may not be aware of the move. This is why it is so important that the ball-handler looks ahead towards the basket at all times. The ball

handler's attention is then focused on the right area of court to see team-mates moving free.

Defence
It is an accepted defensive tactic for the defensive team to pressure the passing lane, but it must be linked with help from defensive team-mates who are marking opponents who are not potential pass receivers. For example, a defender marking a forward in the right-hand corner of court should be able to overplay passes to this forward from the right guard, sure in the knowledge that a team-mate, who is marking the left forward, will have moved under the basket to give cover. Should the right forward break backdoor, the defensive team-mate will be able to step in and help defend the

play. This is called 'weakside' defence.

The idea of weakside defence is that with the ball on one side of the lane, the court can be divided in two by an imaginary line down the middle. This line divides the attacking area into the ball, or strongside, and the weakside of the basket. On the ball side defenders will be marking close and could be denying pass reception. On the weakside the defender will sag off and cover the under-basket area, and will be ready for the backdoor move. Obviously as the ball is passed from one side of the lane to the other so defenders change positions and roles.

The backdoor will frequently be successful, because the defender who initially overplays the passing lane may not react fast enough to

Defending post play—with help from a team-mate

the cut, backdoor to basket. If this occurs the defender should follow the cutter, ignoring the ball, and face him with both arms held high to discourage passes in, or attempt to front him in order to see and intercept the ball.

PICK SCREEN

Attack

The post play is not the only screen that players should be prepared to use and be able to recognise in the game. The basic principle of the screen play is that an attacking player takes up a position which will prevent a defender reaching or maintaining a desired position. Two or more attacking players can work together to free a player from his defender. In the post play the cutter closes the gap between team-mates to create the screen situation. It can also be created by a player, who is to set the screen, converging on his team-mate and stationing himself in such a position that when the team-mate moves his defender will find that he is unable to maintain his defensive position due to the screen. This is usually referred to as a 'pick screen'.

The illustrated pick screen is being used against a pressing defence in the mid-court area. The player with the ball, who is yet to dribble, is closely marked. His team-mate moves and takes up a position facing the ball handler's defender. The ball-handler then drives close to the screening player, causing the defender to check his movements. When setting a pick screen the player should move in facing the

Pick screen being set by white no. 14

opponent to be screened. He should try to use a jump stop in adopting a position with two feet astride the line of the path that the defender will wish to take in following the other attacker. To be legal the screener must be stationary when used by the team-mate.

Pick screen

The advantage of setting the screen facing the team-mate is that it enables the player to see any movement that may be made by the defender and, if necessary, to stop earlier than planned. The use of a jump stop is a clear signal to the team-mate that the screen has been set. The player who will use the screen should fake to go in the opposite direction to the screen, then move close to it and head for basket.

68

Defence

When defending against a team using screens, it is vital that the defender who is being screened realises that it is there. Talking between defensive team-mates must therefore occur. When the defender knows that an opponent is setting a screen he can take action to avoid getting held up on it. The defender will try to go over the top of the screen, which means he moves keeping between his opponent and the screen. Should this not be possible, then he attempts to stay with his opponent by moving behind the screen (known as sliding).

For it to be successful he must have help from his team-mate who steps back, thereby creating space and pulling him through. The disadvantage with sliding is that the attacking player with the ball could make a quick stop and shoot using his team-mate as a front screen. Sliding will be employed when the ball handler is not in a scoring area.

An alternative defence to the slide is for the defenders to switch defensive responsibility (see photographs on page 70). The defender who has been lost on the screen switches to mark the screen by rolling (pivoting on the foot nearest the basket) to stay between his new opponent and the basket; his team-mate moves to cover the

attacking player who has used the screen. The use of switches demands good team-work and understanding between defenders if it is to operate successfully, but unfortunately it may lead to a mis-match in defensive personnel. These three methods of defending against a screen are illustrated in Figure 7.

a) Going over the top

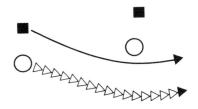

b) Sliding

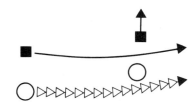

c) Switching

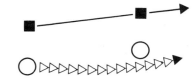

Figure 7 *Defending against a screen*

*Sliding through to defend a
screen play*

69

PICK SCREEN AND ROLL
Attack
The success of the screen may depend on a defender trying to retain defensive responsibility for a particular attacking player. As was seen above, they may switch so that the player moving free is covered. The attacking team still has an additional play to use to counter the switch, that is, for the screener to roll and move to basket. This particular move is illustrated and shows a forward setting a pick screen for a guard who is holding the ball. The forward moves out from the base-line and sets the screen on the defender marking the guard. This

Switching to defend a screen play

Pick and roll

is sometimes called an upscreen. The guard uses the screen to drive for basket and, when the defender marking the forward steps out to deny the guard an unmarked drive to basket, the forward pivots on his inside foot, turning to see the drive being made by his team-mate. This roll by the screener places the defensive player, who has been screened, at the back of the defender who has switched on to the driver. The screener, having rolled, now signals and receives a pass as he moves free towards the basket. The fact that the rolling player should face the driver as he pivots is important and can be applied to other situations in the game. In post play notice that the post player, when he pivots, faces the direction in which his team-mate is moving. Similarly, on the give and go the forward, when he receives the pass from the guard, should pivot to face the basket in such a manner that he continues to face the movement of his team-mate. The one time when a player will turn his back on the team-mate who has given him the ball is if he is reversing on an opponent and driving to basket to take advantage of a mistake by his defender, who was trying to overplay the passing lane.

Defence

The defensive team should endeavour to avoid using switches to counter the screen and roll situation. If a switch is called, then help is essential from defenders on the weakside to cover the driving player. If defensive players take a stance that enables them to see both their opponents and the ball, they will be ready to help those team-mates defend this situation as illustrated previously.

A simple rule for every defender when playing defence should be that 'any opponent driving towards the basket is my man'.

SCREEN OFF THE BALL

Attack

All the screen plays covered so far have involved the screen being set for a ball handler. Players should be prepared to set, and to make use of, a screen that is set off the ball. The post play covered earlier can be used with a third player holding the ball, the cutter losing his opponent on a post and when free, receiving a pass from the ball handler. Another common screen off the ball is the pick screen. The ball handler passes and, instead of following his pass and converging

on his team-mate who has received the ball, moves and sets the screen for a team-mate who does not have the ball. The illustration shows that once the screen is set this team-mate cuts towards the basket, close to the screen, and signals for the pass. It is often used in 'motion offences' to get a player free for a safe pass or quick jump shot.

Defence

If an opponent sets a screen on the defender and the attacking player is outside this shooting range, the simplest way to combat the screen is for the defender to sag, that is, move back towards his basket. This makes it more difficult for a successful screen to be set and gives time for the defender to avoid it. Screen play should be successful only against close-marking defenders, which means that screens off the ball should not work, because the defender marking a player who does not have the ball and who is some way from it should sag and thus be able to avoid any screens that may be set.

Opposite *Screen off the ball*

4 TEAM DEFENCE

The way in which team play in defence is organised will depend upon the application of some basic principles; an ability to perform the techniques covered earlier and an organisation of tactics decided by the coach to counter the strengths of the opposition. In this chapter we discuss some of the basic principles of team defence and consider some basic tactics.

PRINCIPLES OF TEAM DEFENCE

The aim is to obtain possession of the ball without the opponents scoring. The commonest methods of gaining possession will be by obtaining a rebound from a missed shot, or through a violation of the rules by the opponents, or through a passing error by the attacking team. The most important method will be to obtain possession at the rebound from a missed shot. Which shots are liable to miss? Basically, the low percentage shots, which are the long range shots, and the forced shots against close-marking defenders. A crucial ingredient of good team defence is to defend the high percentage scoring area. Defence means pressure and the defending team should try to force an error by pressuring the passer, and by marking passing lanes and potential pass receivers. This pressure on passes can lead to an interception or to the ball being thrown out of court.

It is more difficult to force the attacking team to break a rule, but a few of the time rules do create other opportunities for defensive pressure that can lead to errors and loss of possession. By working hard as a team, it may be possible for the defenders to discourage the opponents from shooting for a long time and so cause them to break the '30 second' rule. The '10 second' and '5 second' rules also present opportunities for defensive pressure to lead to a violation of the rules.

Defending the high percentage scoring area This can be considered under two headings: defending the ball, and defending against a man. When defending the ball, a player will endeavour to prevent shots from and drives and passes into the high percentage scoring area. When defending against an opponent, a defender will try to prevent him receiving the ball in the danger area by overplaying passing lanes, gaining a rebound by blocking out, and gaining a position advantage in the danger area. It must be remembered that the attacking players will vary considerably in their shooting and scoring abilities. What may be a low percentage shooting area for one player could be a high percentage scoring area for another. In defending the high percentage scoring area the defensive team will have those defenders who are furthest from the ball in it to give cover to team-mates.

Matching attacking patterns The attacking team will endeavour to dictate where space will occur on the court; in particular, they will try to keep the under-basket high percentage scoring area clear of too many defenders. The defenders should match their attacking pattern and aim to defend space in the high percentage scoring area. This can be done by using strong/weakside defence, a sagging man-to-man, or a zone defence.

Pressuring to the ball Defence should not be thought of as completely negative, with the defensive team waiting for the attacking team to move. Defenders should take the initiative by trying to pressure their opponents into errors. This can be done by playing defence over the whole court either from a man-to-man formation or by using a zone defence. Players should mark the ball and the close range passing lanes from the ball handler, leaving available only long range passes that defenders will have time to cover. This pressure to the ball should occur in all defences, in that the defenders try to deny passes into the high percentage scoring area.

Organisation There are two basic defensive types, man-to-man defence or zone defence. Man-to-man defence is a style where each player is assigned to defend a specific opponent, regardless of where he goes when on attack. In a zone defence all five defenders work as a team unit and react to the ball, and in so doing each is responsible for an area of the court in which he moves in relation to the movement of the

ball. Both of these types of defence can be played over the whole court.

Communication Members of the defensive team must talk to each other, so that all are aware of attacking moves and defensive commitments. When using a zone defence the ball handler should be marked by one defender, who should tell his team-mate that he has taken responsibility for marking the ball. This enables team-mates to organise their defensive play in relation to the ball.

Importance of individual defence Finally, but most importantly, good team defence depends upon good individual defence; feet and brain must be co-ordinated.

SAGGING MAN-TO-MAN DEFENCE

This is a defensive team tactic by which defenders marking opponents furthest from the ball move away from the attackers towards the basket they are defending. A defender will sag off an opponent who is outside a good shooting range. Although sagging *away* from an opponent, a defender is still responsible for one attacker and will move any time his opponent moves. The defensive player marking the attacker who is standing furthest away from the ball is likely to sag back until he is

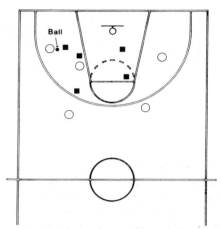

Figure 8 *Sagging man-to-man defence*

standing under the basket: this gives depth to the defence. Using the good passing range of $3\frac{1}{2}$–$4\frac{1}{2}$ metres as a guide, a simple rule of thumb for defenders is that they should be one pace away from a close-marking position for every pass the opponent they are marking is away from the ball.

Details of how to defend some specific attacking plays has already been covered. Using a sagging man-to-man defence the attacking team should find it difficult to pass the ball or drive into the under-basket area and could be forced to rely on longer shots to score points. If the attacking team does not have good long shooters, the advantage in the game will move to the defensive team.

ZONE DEFENCE

A zone defence will start from a basic formation; two commonly used starting formations are the 2–1–2 and the 1–3–1 patterns.

The way in which the coach makes a zone defence work as a unit from these positions can vary. In our opinion the following points should be noted when a zone defence is being used: the ball handler should be marked as though the team were playing man-to-man defence (the next potential receivers of the ball should also be marked man-to-man); the zone should create depth so that the defender marking the ball is covered by another defensive team-mate; defenders should move towards and with the ball; players in the zone should keep their hands up to force passes to the free attacking players to go round the outside of the zone. A zone defence depends for its success on a team's ability to work as a unit, and for this to occur communication is essential. The illustration shows a team using a 2–1–2 zone defence against a 1–3–1 attack.

2–1–2 zone defence in action

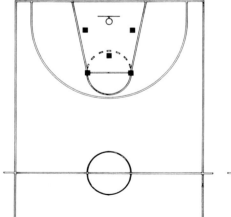

Figure 9 *2–1–2 formation*

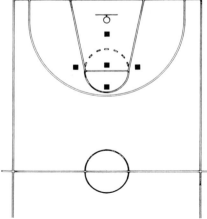

Figure 10 *1–3–1 formation*

PRESSING DEFENCE

A team can use a pressing defence as part of its play tactics. It will do this to try to force the opposition into making mistakes or rushed shots, and will generally frustrate the team attack. A pressing defence can operate from man-to-man or zone style and can be played on the full court, or on three-quarters or half of it. The illustration shows a team playing a man-to-man press. Note that the ball is marked closely and that the defenders have adjusted their position and stance to mark the passing lanes. The defenders marking players who are some distance from the ball do not mark tightly, but act as cover. A pressure defence may also involve attempts by two defenders to 'double-team' the player with the ball. Once trapped, other defenders will

Defensive pressure following a score

adjust their positions to cover the passing lanes.

The strong/weakside defence, already explained, is an example of a pressure defence played half-court. The individual ingredients of pressure defence have been mentioned earlier: see particularly the section concerned with denying pass reception on page 58.

5 TEAM ATTACK

The tactics that a team will use when on attack will depend upon the type of defence encountered. There are a vast number of different methods that can be employed when building up a team attack and which utilise the building blocks of individual and team skills covered earlier in this book. Therefore, we have limited our coverage to the principles of team attacking play and some examples of how the basic skills and principles can be applied.

PRINCIPLES OF TEAM ATTACK

Aim

The main aim of the attacking team is to retain possession of the ball until an opportunity for a good shot is created. There will occasionally be times when the subsidiary aim of retaining possession and consuming time is more important, for example when a team is one point in the lead and there are only 25 seconds left to play. As the rules require a team to shoot within 30 seconds, the team only need to retain possession to win and so under no circumstances should they shoot—even uncontested lay-up shots have been missed. While a team has possession of the ball the opponents cannot score.

Use of Space

The space between attacking team-mates is an important ingredient of team attack. This space will be influenced by the good passing range of $3\frac{1}{2}$–$4\frac{1}{2}$ metres and the distance from the basket that accurate shots can be taken. At this range attacking team-mates can make quick, safe passes and the defensive team will be forced to mark on a one-to-one basis. The space between attacking team-mates will give the player with the ball room to drive to basket without having to cope with more than one defender, and thus assists not only with driving plays but also with cutting plays. The good passing range could be looked upon as a support range, in that team-mates at this distance support each other, but note that because basketball is a fast passing game attacking formations create situations in which some players on court support team-mates who do not have the ball. This is a good policy: it keeps the defenders occupied and places the attacking players in an advantageous position should the ball be passed. The three lane fast break covered later is a good example of attacking players supporting each other. This range of $3\frac{1}{2}$–$4\frac{1}{2}$ metres can be looked upon as a divergent situation on attack, with screen plays being the convergent situation. Since the building blocks of individual and team skills have already been discussed earlier, we have limited our coverage here to principles of team attacking play and to some examples of how the basic skills and principles can be applied.

Threat

Ideally, a player on attack in his front court should, when he receives a pass, be a scoring threat. Should he move out of scoring range he will become less of a threat to the defenders and so easier to mark. Another point to mention under the heading of threat is that the attacking team should endeavour to penetrate the defence by moving the ball or players towards the basket. This penetration can create problems for the defensive team; for example, the defender marking the attacking player who has passed into the under-basket area may not be able to see both his opponent and the ball. The movement the attacking team uses will create scoring chances. The form that the movement takes could depend upon the defence being employed, with emphasis on player movement against man-to-man defence and upon ball movement when attacking a zone defence. These are for emphasis only. Opportunities will occur when player movement is the most appropriate method of creating a scoring chance against a zone defence.

Organisation

The amount of organisation in a team's attacking play will depend upon the coach. He may wish to use patterns that players have learned during training sessions, or he may give his team a basic formation and want them to play freely from these positions. These extremes of approach have limitations: playing freely, for example, makes it more difficult for all members of the team to know what is happening.

Creating Scoring Opportunities

Three basic methods of creating a scoring situation can be isolated. These are:

☐ the player with the ball manoeuvres to free himself for a shot;

☐ a player without the ball moves free and then receives a pass and shoots; and

☐ a screen situation is used to enable an attacking player to lose the defender who is responsible for marking him.

All these methods of creating a scoring situation have been covered earlier, see pages 44–53 and 62–73.

TEAM ATTACK VERSUS MAN-TO-MAN DEFENCE (MOTION OFFENCE)

A simple team attack to use against a man-to-man defence is what is called a motion offence, sometimes termed the passing game. In this style of attacking play there is no predetermined order of movement of either players or of the basketball. It is a freelance attack, with players operating to tactics decided by the coach. The emphasis is on ball and player movement, and the dribble is discouraged. With little dribble all attacking players are in 'motion', looking to receive a pass. The 'rules' of operation will make use of the basic team plays we have covered in Chapter 3. This style of attack leaves the players considerable freedom of action; such freedom makes it very difficult for the opposition to scout the team and understand exactly what is happening. At a very simple level the attacking team could use a horse-shoe formation, with the following rules of operation:

Look ahead
Pass ahead
Move ahead
Spread out

This very simple team play should give the team on attack a number

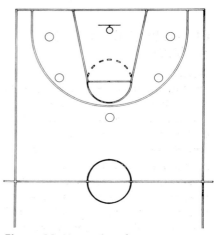

Figure 11 *Horse-shoe formation*

of give and go and post plays to move a player free, and is very suitable for use with inexperienced players.

A more sophisticated team play using a motion offence could be a 1–3–1 formation. This could also be considered a formation in which the team has two players working on attack in the pivot area, one at high post, i.e. close to the free-throw line, and the other at low post, i.e. close to the base line. The other three players play outside the key.

The rules of operation for this formation could be as follows:

All players

☐ Move to meet the pass.

☐ Move after passing the ball, either to the basket or to screen away.

☐ Screen away from the ball.

☐ Balance the offence, that is, maintain a $3\frac{1}{2}$–$4\frac{1}{2}$ metre spacing between players on the perimeter of the offence.

☐ Penetrate the ball to the high percentage scoring areas; in particular look to pass to a pivot player.

High post

☐ Start with interchange with low post.

☐ Remain one pass away from the ball at all times, even if this means stepping out of the lane.

☐ When the ball is received look for the low post.

☐ When no pass is possible to the low post look to pass to the side away from the passer.

Low post

☐ Play weakside.

☐ When the high post receives a pass, roll to basket.

☐ When the high post moves low, the low post moves to a high position.

PATTERN ATTACK

The attack that follows is an example of a patterned attack which could be used against a man-to-man defence. This type of attack gives the players less freedom and requires them to create and recognise scoring opportunities that occur as they work through the pattern. The starting floor formation is a 2–1–2 formation with two guards, two forwards and one pivot. From the basic formation the attacking team moves to create an overload triangle in one corner. The pattern is illustrated in Figures 12–17. This type of pattern play makes use of a number of screen situations and will involve the players learning their role in the pattern. Obviously many other options deriving from it are possible; for example, in the last play a pick screen and roll could be employed. When the attack breaks down and

a scoring chance is not created the players return to the starting position, reset, and then start the pattern again, or rotate the players so that the attack can be initiated on the other side of the court.

TEAM ATTACK VERSUS ZONE DEFENCE

With each defender in a zone defence being responsible for a particular zone in the formation, the defence is not complete until all five defenders are in their places. For this reason the first attacking weapon to use is the fast break. Only when the fast break has not been successful will other weaknesses in the zone defence be attacked. To exploit them the attacking team will have to display patience to create an opening. Since each defender is responsible for an area on the floor, there will be points in the defence at which two defenders' areas of responsibility meet. These are points of weakness in the zone defence, because the defenders may be unsure about which of them is to mark a player at the gap. Therefore, attacking players need to be stationed so they attack the gaps between defenders. The diagrams show two different line-ups of players attacking different zone defences; note that where the defence has two defenders at the front of the zone

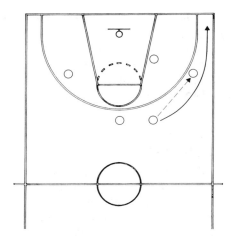

Figure 12 *Guard passes to forward and moves to the corner*

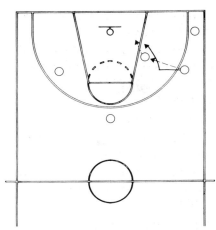

Figure 13 *Forward looks to cut off the post; the ball could also be passed to the guard in the corner for the guard to use the post*

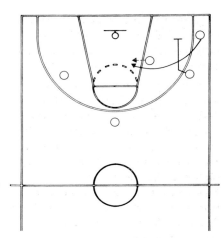

Figure 14 *The forward may also set a screen for the guard who cuts off both forward and post play*

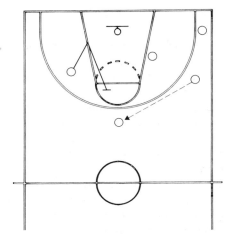

Figure 15 *When the side line triangle has not created a shot the ball can be passed to the second guard*

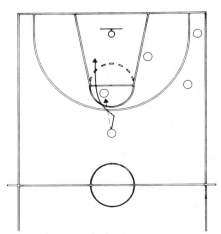

Figure 16 *The second guard looks to pass to the second forward, who has come to high post position, and to cut off the post*

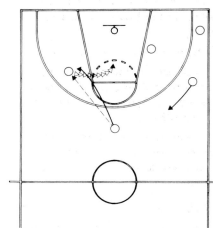

Figure 17 *As an alternative, the second guard can pass to the second forward and set a pick screen for him to use*

then the attack line up with one guard, and against a zone with one defender at the front the attack use two guards. The formations in Figures 18 and 19 show another point about zone attack, which is that attacking players are spread wide.

A further weakness of the zone defence is that because they defend and move with the ball, they can be outmanoeuvred by rapid passing—the ball can be moved faster than defenders can move. For example, in Figure 19, if the ball is with player 03 and defender X1 comes to cover, a pass to 02 will bring X3 to defend and leave 01 free for a high percentage shot. This is also an example of attacking from behind the zone.

Most zone defences concentrate defenders in the high percentage area under the basket, and

Using a front screen to create a shooting opportunity

because of this a method of beating a zone is to increase the area of court that is a high percentage scoring area for your team, thus shooting and scoring over the top of the zone. A front screen can be used to give an attacking player more space and time for a shot over the zone. In the illustration the player in the left-hand corner is taking a shot over a front screen being set by a team-mate. The attacking team will frequently find that the zone defenders will allow a player in the corner of the court to move closer to basket for a shot than they would an attacking player to the front of the basket. The front screen shows another move which can be used against a zone defence and that is to create an

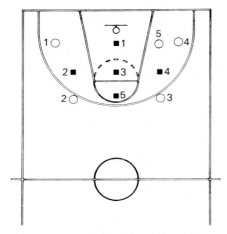

Figure 18 *Zone attack – 2 guards*

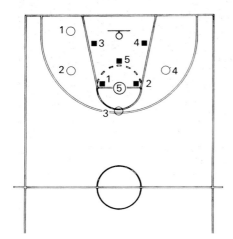

Figure 19 *Zone attack – 1 guard*

'overload' against one defender by moving two or more attackers into his zone.

The attacking team will need to develop an inside game to be able to beat a zone defence consistently. This can be achieved if an attacking player stationed on the weakside (that is, on the side of the court away from the ball) sees a space in the zone and steps into the middle of the restricted area. If he receives the ball, he should turn to face the basket, looking for a shot, or as the defenders move towards him he should make a pass to a team-mate who is free just outside the zone. Here the zone is being attacked from behind and can be very effective because the zone defenders will be focusing their attention on the ball.

TEAM ATTACK VERSUS FULL COURT PRESSING DEFENCES

Since the aim of a press is to change the rhythm and force poor shots and passes, when attacking a pressing defence the attacking team should keep calm. Against full court pressure the attacking team will want to move the ball into their front court and then go into their regular team attack. However, if the attacking team relax after moving the ball across the centre line, the defensive team can still cause problems. Therefore, against a press the attacking team should aim to take the ball to the basket or, if this is not possible, to a player on the baseline.

Against a man-to-man press it is usual to give the ball to the best dribbler and clear space to allow him to go one-versus-one against his opponent and to move the ball to the front court.

If the opponents are employing a zone press, they will be trying to double team the ball handler, and a dribble or pass to a player who is at the very corner of the court will make this easier. The attacking team against a zone defence should:

☐ Limit the dribble, pass the ball and keep it moving.

☐ When passing in from the baseline after a score, move away from the basket before passing.

☐ Spread the defence so that they have a greater area to cover.

☐ Move to meet the ball. This will prevent many interceptions.

☐ Aim to move the ball forwards, not laterally.

☐ Use the taller players as receivers in the middle of the court. They should move down court and then break back to receive the pass.

☐ Avoid receiving passes near the centre line to prevent front and rear court violations.

☐ Fake before passing.

☐ Do not panic.

FAST BREAK

Possession of the ball is the difference between being on the attack and being on defence. There needs to be immediate reaction to any change of possession. The team that has gained possession should, if they can, attack immediately whilst the defence is at a disadvantage. The fast break is normally the team's initial attack. They should aim to take the ball down court into a scoring position in the front court before the opponents have had time to recover and to organise their defence.

To prevent the attacking team gaining an advantage the defensive team should respond to the change of possession quickly and defensively by fast breaking, and should move to their defensive positions rapidly.

Attacking Fast Break

A fast break attack can be considered in three phases: the outlet pass to get the break started, the effort to fill lanes as the ball is taken down court, and taking advantage of the first good shot created.

Getting the Break Started

At the start of the break the reaction of the team to the change of possession is vital. Two common situations that occur during the game when a fast break can be started are following a defensive rebound and after a score by the opposition. The pass out from these two situations needs to be developed.

Outlet Pass after a Score

After the score the player nearest the ball should quickly take it one step off court (one foot is sufficient if the other foot is lifted) and immediately pass the ball in court. The player making the pass from out-of-bounds throws the ball, often using a one-hand pass, into a space for a team-mate who has broken free. The player taking the ball out must operate at speed, for the time that he uses in stepping off court and throwing the ball in will give the opponents the opportunity to move back on defence and prevent the new attacking team gaining a numerical advantage at the end of their break. In the

Starting a fast break after a scored basket

84

illustration the ball is received at the side of the court, but outlet passes vary depending upon the tactics employed by the coach. The long ball may be used when the coach has players with the appropriate physical ability and involves releasing a player as soon as a shot goes up.

Outlet Pass from a Rebound

Upon gathering a defensive rebound the new attacking team should aim to pass the ball from the congested under-basket area as quickly as possible. As the rebounder gathers the ball a team-mate should break to a position at the side (about level with the free-throw lane) where he receives the outlet pass from the rebounder. The outlet pass to the side has the advantage of clearing the middle of the court, which could well be congested.

If the rebounder finds that he has no immediate opportunity for a pass, he should look to use a power dribble from under basket straight down the court, thus clearing space for a pass to a team-mate who has moved down court.

Filling the Lanes

Once the outlet pass has been made and the ball cleared from the basket area, the attacking team need to capitalise on any advantage gained.

If the opponents have been very slow moving back to defence on the loss of possession, the player who receives the outlet pass may be able to drive all the way down court for an uncontested shot. Even if this does occur, team-mates should not just stand back and watch. The player may miss the shot at basket.

A team will be able to break fast successfully if all its members strive to be involved, aiming to move quickly down court so that they have a chance to out-number the opponents at the end of the break.

As the team breaks down court, the players should try to fill three lanes: one player goes down the middle and the other two go down each side of the court. This use of width in attack poses problems for the defence. As the ball crosses the half-way line into their front court the attacking team aim to have the

Figure 20 *The fast break*

Below *Starting a fast break from a rebound*

Photographs on page 87
Final phase of a fast break

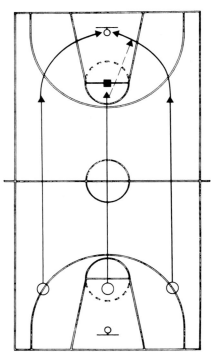

player with the ball in the middle of the court. With two team-mates having gone into the outside lanes, the attack has now filled three lanes of attack. Bringing the ball down court, the attacking team may either inter-pass the ball or leave one player to dribble it all the way. Having established a position in one of the lanes, the fast breaking players try to retain their lane position. To switch lanes can confuse team-mates. Figure 20 shows the filling of the three lanes on the fast break.

Final Phase of the Fast Break

As the attacking team bring the ball into the scoring area, the ball should be under the control of the player in the middle lane. If he can, this player should attempt to go all the way to the basket and only pass off when his forward progress is blocked. With the ball in the middle of the court, there is the option of a pass to either side. If the progress of the player in the middle is blocked, he should try to penetrate to the side of a defender, looking to shoot or pass, or come to a stop at the free-throw lane. As they reach an area near the head of the free-throw lane, his team-mates, who have filled the outside lanes, should cut towards the basket signalling for a pass.

DEFENCE AGAINST A FAST BREAK

To stop opponents gaining a numerical advantage through the use of a fast break the defenders should aim to delay the outlet pass, by quick defensive breaking; and if the opponents do succeed in gaining a numerical advantage, they should try to delay the shot.

To delay the start of the break the attacking rebounder should endeavour to mark the opposing player who has rebounded and stop him from making a quick outlet pass.

Delaying the start of a fast break

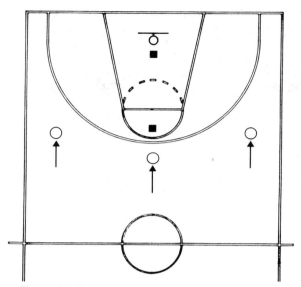

Figure 21 *Tandem*

Tandem defence when defence is outnumbered

Should the opponents succeed with the outlet pass the defence should recover to the under-basket area as quickly as possible, and force them to take the long shot or to make additional passes that will give team-mates time to recover. Defensive organisation requires that two players recover quickly, setting up in a tandem formation— one under the basket and the other in front. The defender at the front of the tandem aims to stop the ball, thus forcing a pass to the side. As the ball goes to the side the defender under the basket moves out to mark the ball handler, and the player who was at the front of the tandem moves back to cover the under-basket area and to stop the pass across to the player on the opposite side. With this organisation the defenders are defending out from the basket, preventing the lay-up shot even if it gives a jump shot, and defending the jump shot even if it gives a long range shot. Should an attacker drive past the front player the rear defender is able to cover to prevent penetration and, taking up a good defensive position, to draw a charge foul on the driving player.

SPECIAL SITUATIONS

During the game a number of situations occur to which players must be alert. These are jump balls, free throws and 'out-of-bounds'. Although a team may use some special tactics on these occasions, the following general points should be considered.

Jump Ball

At a jump ball a player should mark in a position between his opponent and the basket defended. Using this formation both jumpers will find they have one safe tipping area where two team-mates stand side by side. The tip should be directed between these two players. Remember that players can cross the restraining circle as soon as the ball has been tipped. Prior to the tip the players should concentrate on the jumpers, being particularly alert to their hands on the ball. When the jump ball is to be held at a free-throw line, both teams should move quickly to gain the position on the circle closest to the basket. If an attacking player can gain this position he will be a considerable threat, for should he catch the ball he can step either to left or right on a move to basket.

Free Throw

At the free throw the defensive team take the first spaces on either side of the lane and the attacking team the second spaces. The defending team should ensure that one player is lined up ready to

move into the lane to block out the shooter should the last free throw miss. In addition to those players who have lined up, the defending team should have a player in a position away from the lane at the side of the court, ready to receive the outlet pass to start the team's fast break.

Out-of-Bounds

In the section on fast break it was mentioned that, following a basket, a player should quickly take the ball out-of-bounds for a quick throw in. It would be dangerous to use this on every out-of-bounds throw in. There are 5 seconds in

which to release the ball and the team with possession should be prepared to use this time. To organise an out-of-bounds play to free a player for a safe pass is particularly important when a thirty-seconds period has almost expired. The defensive team should remember that they have five players on the court to the opposition's four. The spare player may be used to front the opposing pivot and to prevent the pass in from out-of-bounds or to pressure the out-of-bounds ball.

Line-up for a free throw

90

Zone defence

GLOSSARY OF BASKETBALL TERMS

Originally published in the English Basket Ball Association's Coaching Booklet, *A Guide for the Potential Basketball Coach*, this is reproduced by kind permission of the EBBA.

Basketball like other sports has its own 'jargon' which is used to describe certain aspects of playing the game. Often a number of different names are given to the same action and, of course, many terms have their origin in the rules of the game. Most of the terms originating from the rules have been omitted but where they are given this point has been noted. Where more than one term is used the most popular one has been defined. It is hoped that through the use of a standard terminology communication and understanding will be improved between coaches, players and officials.

Alive offensive player who has the ball, but who has not dribbled.

Assist a pass to an open team-mate that results in an immediate score.

Back court that half of the court which contains a team's defensive basket.

Backdoor a term used to describe a cut by an offensive player towards the basket to the side of the defensive player away from the ball. It is mainly used when the offensive player is being overplayed or when the defence turns to look at the ball or in another direction.

Ball control game a type of offensive play that emphasises maintaining possession of the ball until a good shot is possible.

Ball side the side of the defensive formation close to the ball. *See also* Help side.

Baseline drive a drive (*q.v.*) made close to the offensive end line of the court.

Blocking 'is personal contact which impedes the progress of an opponent who is not in possession of the ball. *See* Rules, Article 80.

Blocking out (*Blocking off*) (*Boxing out*) (*Cutting out*) the positioning of a player in such a manner as to prevent an opposing player from moving to the basket to gain a rebound.

Box and one a term used to describe a combination defence (*q.v.*) with four men playing a zone defence (*q.v.*) in a square formation (i.e. 2-2) with one man out chasing a particular opponent.

Break the rapid movement of a player to a space where he hopes to receive a pass.

Brush-off (*Brush off screen*) to cause one's opponent to run into a third player, thus 'losing' him momentarily.

Buttonhook to move in one direction, and then to turn sharply and double-back.

Centre the name of one of the positions in the team, usually the tallest player. The pivot or post play (*q.v.*).

Charging a personal foul caused by a player making bodily contact by running into an opponent. Usually committed by an offensive player.

Chaser a defender whose duty is to harass the offensive players, usually the front man or men in a zone defence (*q.v.*).

Circulation a player's movements about the court on offence.

Clear out an offensive manoeuvre in which players vacate an area of court to isolate one offensive player and one defensive player. The offensive player may then attempt to score against his opponent who has no defensive team-mates close enough to help him.

Combination defence a team defence where some of the team play zone defence (*q.v.*) and others man-to-man defence (*q.v.*).

Continuity play a team offensive system in which men move to one position and then executing in a regular order, executing pre-planned play options in an endeavour to create a scoring opportunity. The offensive players' movements on court are so planned that it is not necessary to set up (*q.v.*) the offensive pattern after each play option has been attempted. The positioning of players after one play option has been tried is used as the starting position for the next option.

Control basketball (*Possession basketball*) a style of play in which a team deliberately makes sure of every pass and only shoots when there is a very high percentage chance of scoring.

Controlling the boards gaining the majority of the rebounds.

Cut a quick movement by an offensive player without the ball to gain an advantage over the defence, usually directed towards the basket.

Cutter a player who cuts (*q.v.*) or breaks (*q.v.*).

Dead an offensive player who has used his dribble.

Diamond and one a term used to describe a combination defence (*q.v.*), with four men playing a zone defence (*q.v.*) in a diamond formation (i.e. 1-2-1) with one man out chasing the ball or marking a particular opponent.

Drill a repetitive practice designed to improve one or more particular fundamental skills or team combinations.

Drive the movement of an offensive player while aggressively dribbling towards the basket in an attempt to score.

Double team when two defensive players mark one opponent with the ball, usually a temporary measure (*see* Trap).

Dunk a shot in which a jumping player puts the ball down into the opponent's basket from above.

Fake (*Feint*) a movement made with the aim of deceiving an opponent.

Fall-away a method of performing certain shots and passes in which the player with the ball moves in one direction as the ball moves in another.

Fast break (*Quick break*) a fast offence that attempts to advance the ball to the front court before the defence is organised, with the object of achieving numerical superiority to give a good shot.

Feed to pass the ball to a team-mate who is in a scoring position.

Feint *see* Fake.

Floor play used to describe the movements on the court of players of either team.

Fouled out being required to leave the game after committing five fouls.

Foul line free-throw line.

Forward the name of one of the positions in the team. The forwards play on offence in the area of court, either on the right- or left-hand side, between the restricted area (*q.v.*) and the side lines.

Free ball (*Loose ball*) a ball which, although in play, is not in the possession of either team.

Freelance an unstructured type of offence where players take advantage of whatever offensive opportunities arise.

Freezing the ball (*Stall*) the action of a team in possession of the ball which attempts to retain possession without an attempt to score. Limited to 30 seconds and often used late in the game in an effort to protect a slight lead.

Front court that half of the court which contains the basket a team is attacking.

Fronting the post guarding the post player (*q.v.*) in front rather than between him and the basket. A defensive tactic aiming to prevent a good post player from receiving the ball close to the basket.

Front screen a screen set up by an offensive player between a team-mate and his opponent.

Full-court press a pressing defence which operates throughout the whole court and not merely in the defender's back court (*q.v.*). *See* Press.

Fundamentals the basic skills of the game, necessary as a background for all team play.

Give and go an offensive manoeuvre in which a player passes the ball to a team-mate and cuts (*q.v.*) towards basket for a return pass.

Guard (*Playmaker*) (*Quarter-back*) the name of one of the positions on the team, usually played by the shorter players, who on offence will play in the area of court between the centre line and the free-throw line extended to the side-lines.

Half-court press a pressing defence which operates in a team's back court.

Held ball is 'declared when two players of opposing teams have one or both hands firmly on the ball'. *See* Rules, Article 55.

Help side the side of the defensive formation away from the ball, the weak side (*q.v.*). A defender on the help side will move to the ball to give depth to the defence and in particular will be prepared to help the team-mate marking the ball handler.

High a position played by an offensive player who plays in the area of court away from the end line near to the free-throw line.

In line the basic man-to-man defensive position 'in line' between the opponent and the basket being defended.

Inside (i) in the under basket area; (ii) between the perimeter of the defence and the basket they are defending; (iii) 'inside' the key (*q.v.*).

Jump ball 'a jump ball takes place when the official tosses the ball between two opposing players'. *See* Rules, Article 26.

Key (*Keyhole*) the restricted area (*q.v.*), including the circle, derived from the original keyhole shape.

Lane *see* Restricted area.

Lead pass a pass thrown ahead of the intended receiver so that he can catch the ball on the move and maintain his speed.

Low a position held by an offensive player operating in the area of court near to the end line or basket.

Man-to-man defence a style of defence where each player is assigned to guard a specific opponent, regardless of where he goes in his offensive manoeuvres.

Motion offence a style of offensive play with no predetermined order of movement of players or the ball. The offence is based upon constant movement of all five players. Players look to use basic individual and team plays to take advantage of defence errors. Some order may be given to the movements by the coach introducing rules of action, e.g. every time a pass is made the passer looks to cut to basket or set a screen away from the ball.

Out-of-bounds the area outside the legal playing court, i.e. outside the inside edge of the lines marking the side lines and the end lines.

Off line a variation of 'in line' defence (*q.v.*) in which the defender takes up a position slightly to one side of his opponent but still between the opponent and the basket. The aim is to reduce the opponent's offensive options.

One on one (*1 v. 1*) the situation in which one offensive player attacks one defensive player.

Options alternative offensive manoeuvres that can occur in a game situation.

Outlet pass the first pass made after a defensive rebound (*q.v.*), usually made to a player stationed near to the closest sideline of the court and used to initiate a fast break (*q.v.*).

Outside (i) nearer the sideline of the court; (ii) between the sideline and the perimeter of the defence; (iii) 'outside' the key (*q.v.*).

Overload outnumber.

Overtime the extra period(s) played after the expiration of the second half of a game in which the score has been tied. Play is continued for an extra period of five minutes or as many such periods of five minutes as may be necessary to break the tie.

Pass and cut *see* Give and go.

Passing game a motion offence (*q.v.*) with the emphasis on passing the ball with little or no use of the dribble.

Passing lane space through which a pass is possible. New passing lanes may be opened by signals or player movement.

Pattern the predetermined positional formation adopted by an offensive team prior to their initiating offensive manoeuvres. Common patterns are 1–3–1 and 2–3.

Pattern play offensive plays initiated from fixed and predetermined court positions.

Pick (*Side-screen*) a screen (*q.v.*) set at the side of a team-mate's opponent.

Pick and roll a side screen followed by a pivot towards the basket by the player

who has set the screen; useful against a switching man-to-man defence.

Pivot (i) 'a pivot takes place when a player who is holding the ball steps once or more than once in any direction with the same foot, the other foot called the pivot foot, being kept at its point of contact with the floor'. *See* Rules, Article 52. (ii) Another name for a Post player (*q.v.*).

Play a term used to describe a series of movements of players and/or the ball on court; mainly used for offensive manoeuvres.

Playmaker a player who is adept at setting up situations that will give team-mates a scoring opportunity. *See also* Guard.

Post (i) *see* Post player; (ii) an offensive manoeuvre in which a player takes up a position usually with his back to the basket he is attacking, thus providing a target to receive a pass and/or act as a rear screen (*q.v.*) to enable team-mates to run their opponents into the post.

Post player usually the tallest player in the team who operates on offence in an area near the sides of, and occasionally in, the free-throw lane and close to the basket. He is stationed there for scoring purposes and to feed cutters (*q.v.*), and is a player around whom the offensive team pivot. He is, therefore, sometimes called a pivot player.

Press a defensive attempt to force the opposing team into making some kind of error and thus losing possession of the ball. It is accomplished usually by aggressive defence, double teaming (*q.v.*) or harassing the ball handler with attempts to tie up (*q.v.*) the ball. The press can be applied full court, half court or any other fractional part of the playing area and can be based on either man-to-man or zone (*q.v.*) principles.

Quarterback *see* Playmaker *or* Guard. A term derived from American Football.

Quick break *see* Fast break.

Rebound a term used to describe the actual retrieving of the ball as it rebounds from the backboard of the ring after an unsuccessful shot. Offensive rebound therefore means gaining the rebound from the team's offensive basket (i.e. the one it is attacking). Defensive rebound is retrieving the ball from the team's defensive basket (i.e. the basket it is defending).

Rebound triangle a term used to describe the positioning of a group of three defenders who form a triangle around the basket after a shot has been attempted. Their aim is to cover the probable positions of the ball, should a rebound occur, and to prevent an opponent from gaining a good position from which to collect the rebound.

Restraining circles circles with a diameter of 3.60 metres (12 feet) located in the centre of the court and at the free-throw lines.

Restricted areas 'The restricted areas shall be spaces marked in the court which are limited by the end lines, the free-throw lines and by lines which originate at the end lines, their outer edges being 3 metres from the midpoints of the end lines, and terminate at the end of the free throw lines.' *See* Rules, Article 7.

Reverse (*Roll*) a change of direction in which the offensive player endeavours to free himself from a close marking defender. The change of direction is executed after a move towards the defender and a pivot, so that the offensive player turns his back on his opponent and then moves off in the new direction.

Safety man an offensive player who plays in the guard position with the aim of defending against possible fast breaks on loss of possession and receiving a pass when an offensive play breaks down.

Sag when a defender moves away from his opponent towards the basket he is defending.

Sagging defence a team defensive tactic by which the defenders furthest from the ball sag away from their opponents towards the basket to help their team-mates and cover the high percentage scoring area.

Screen a screen occurs when an offensive player attempts to prevent a defender from reaching a desired position or maintaining his defensive position. The screen is intended to impede the progress of the defender so that the offensive player he is marking has an unimpeded shot or a clear path to basket.

Scrimmage a practice game.

Set play (i) a repetitive, pre-arranged form of offence; (ii) a play (*q.v.*) executed to predetermined and rehearsed moves which, when applied at certain set situations in the game, is intended to result in a favourable scoring chance (the set situations are usually out-of-bounds, jump ball or the free-throw situation).

Set up the action of establishing an offensive pattern (*q.v.*) or the defensive organisation.

Slow break a deliberate attack against a defence that is set up (*q.v.*).

Slide when a defensive player, in order to prevent himself being screened, moves (as he follows his own opponent) between a team-mate and that team-mate's opponent.

Stall *see* Freezing the ball.

Steal to take the ball away from an opponent.

Strong side refers to the side of the court on which the offensive team has the ball (at any one time).

Switch a defensive manoeuvre in which two defenders exchange defensive responsibilities by changing the men they are guarding. It usually occurs during a screen situation in which one of the defenders can no longer guard his man because of the screen.

System a team's basic offensive and defensive plays.

Tie up a defensive situation in which the defenders, through their defensive tactics, gain a held ball (*q.v.*) or a five seconds violation situation.

Tip the momentary catching and pushing of the ball towards the basket, executed by an offensive rebounder in an attempt to score from an offensive rebound (*q.v.*) while he is still in the air.

Tip off the centre jump-ball at the start of play.

Trailer an offensive player who follows behind the ball handler.

Trap a 'double team' (*q.v.*) in which two defenders attempt to stop a dribbler and prevent him from making a successful pass.

Transposition occurs after the change of possession as a team moves from offence to defence, and vice versa.

Turnover the loss of ball possession without there having been an attempt by the offensive team to shoot at basket.

Weak-side the opposite side of the court to the strongside (*q.v.*), that is, away from the ball.

Zone defence a team's defensive tactic in which the five defensive players react to the ball and, in so doing, are each responsible for an area of the court in which they move in relation to the movements of the ball.

INDEX